First Time

A Musical

Book by
Kirk Foster and John Gardiner

Lyrics by
Kirk Foster

Music by
Kirk Foster and Paul Sabey

Samuel French – London
New York – Sydney – Toronto – Hollywood

Copyright © 1986 by Kirk Foster (book and lyrics) and
John Gardiner (book)
All Rights Reserved

FIRST TIME is fully protected under the copyright laws of the British Commonwealth, including Canada, the United States of America, and all other countries of the Copyright Union. All rights, including professional and amateur stage productions, recitation, lecturing, public reading, motion picture, radio broadcasting, television and the rights of translation into foreign languages are strictly reserved.

ISBN 978-0-573-08073-9

www.samuelfrench.co.uk
www.samuelfrench.com

FOR AMATEUR PRODUCTION ENQUIRIES

**UNITED KINGDOM AND WORLD
EXCLUDING NORTH AMERICA**
plays@samuelfrench.co.uk
020 7255 4302/01

Each title is subject to availability from Samuel French, depending upon country of performance.

CAUTION: Professional and amateur producers are hereby warned that *FIRST TIME* is subject to a licensing fee. Publication of this play does not imply availability for performance. Both amateurs and professionals considering a production are strongly advised to apply to the appropriate agent before starting rehearsals, advertising, or booking a theatre. A licensing fee must be paid whether the title is presented for charity or gain and whether or not admission is charged.

No one shall make any changes in this title for the purpose of production. No part of this book may be reproduced, stored in a retrieval system, or transmitted in any form, by any means, now known or yet to be invented, including mechanical, electronic, photocopying, recording, videotaping, or otherwise, without the prior written permission of the publisher. No one shall upload this title, or part of this title, to any social media websites.

The right of Kirk Foster and John Gardiner to be identified as authors of this work has been asserted in accordance with Section 77 of the Copyright, Designs and Patents Act 1988.

FIRST TIME

First performed at the Queen Mother Theatre, Hitchin, Hertfordshire, on 4th September 1985, by the Kads Theatre Company.

The Company:

Kirk Foster	Sarah Baker
Gerard Doyle	Angie Guy
Keith Swainston	Paula Tappenden
Michael Flintoff	Selina Jones
Glen Davies	Jo Russ
Tim Young	Janette Frazer
Mark Lingwood	Judith Ellis
Gary Bowman	Marcia Hewitt
Iain Leary	Janette Swallow

Music arranged and performed by Paul Sabey

Directed by Kirk Foster

CHARACTERS

FIRST HALF

Paul (Marvin's Dad)	Mr Turner, the teacher
Sally (Marvin's Mum)	Careers Officer
Asthmatic Old Man	Doreen, a secretary
Business Man	Betty
Trendy Lefty Lady	Sandra
Mrs P, an office cleaner	Rene
Another Man	Ray
Another Woman	May
Emily ⎫ two old spinsters	Debbie
Violet ⎭	Dora
Policeman	Pat
Policewoman	Mayor's entourage
Docker	Singer
Nurses	Backing group
St John's Ambulance Men	Marvin's Girl
Surgeons	Girl-Friend
Doctors	Two boys
Matrons	Julie
Three Mothers	Old Gertie
Marvin	Tina
Sid	The Narrator
Tom	Jackie Boy, the Butler
June	Esmerelda
Brenda	Alucard's Mother
Gloria	Alucard
Nutty Norman	Two asylum Assistants
Nutty Norman's Gang	Two Maids

Additional SECOND HALF characters

Girl with big feet	Sonia
Girl with hunch back	Stephen
"Camp" guy	Old Lady
Vicar	Doctor
Julie's Dad	Female Patient
Julie's Mum	Satan
Tall thin bridesmaid	Judge
Short tubby bridesmaid	Miss Twee
Photographer	Jury
Organist	Dobbs
Jane	Syms
Sarah	Cleaner
	PC Matthews
	Voices from the past
	God

FIRST TIME

Production Notes

Page

First Half
First Time (song)	1
First Child (sketch)	2
Baby (song)	9
First Fag (sketch)	11
Can You Remember? (song)	17
First Job (sketch)	18
First Night (sketch)	22
First Night Blues (song)	26
First Glance (song)	27
First Kiss (sketch)	29
A Woman (song)	34
First Bite (sketch)	35
Jugular Blues (song)	42

Second Half
First Time (Reprise—song)	45
First Time I Saw You (song)	45
First Wife	47
We Are Just Beginning (song)	51
First Family Christmas (sketch)	52
After the Party (song)	57
First Aid (sketch)	58
Taking Time (song)	61
First Medical (sketch)	61
First to Fall (song)	63
First Offence (sketch)	64
First Death (sketch)	71
First to Fall (Reprise—song)	73
First Time (Reprise—song)	73

Technical Plots 78

The show runs for approximately 110 minutes

The music is available from Samuel French Ltd as is a demo showcase cassette of the music

A licence issued by Samuel French Ltd to perform this play only extends to the music specially written for the play. If additional copyright music, as specified in the text, is used the notice printed below on behalf of the Performing Right Society should be carefully read.

The following statement concerning the use of music is printed here on behalf of the Performing Right Society Ltd, by whom it was supplied

The permission of the owner of the performing right in copyright music must be obtained before any public performance may be given, whether in conjunction with a play or sketch or otherwise, and this permission is just as necessary for amateur performances as for professional. The majority of copyright musical works (other than oratorios, musical plays and similar dramatico-musical works) are controlled in the British Commonwealth by the PERFORMING RIGHT SOCIETY LTD, 29–33 BERNERS STREET, LONDON W1P 4AA.

The Society's practice is to issue licences authorizing the use of its repertoire to the proprietors of premises at which music is publicly performed, or, alternatively, to the organizers of musical entertainments, but the Society does not require payment of fees by performers as such. Producers or promoters of plays, sketches, etc., at which music is to be performed, during or after the play or sketch, should ascertain whether the premises at which their performances are to be given are covered by a licence issued by the Society and if they are not, should make application to the Society for particulars as to the fee payable.

PRODUCTION NOTES

The Set
This show is best presented on an open stage. There is no scenery. On the cyclorama cloth there is a huge staff with gigantic notes painted on. The company may choose any of the opening notes and clefs from one of the *First Time* songs. The eye should be flooded with different colours according to the mood of each scene. The floor ideally should be on three levels, the highest level quite narrow and upstage, the second level slightly wider but the major playing area should be downstage and spacious.

Depending on the number you use in your company there should be that number of chairs on the set, arranged at different levels. The chairs can either be uniform colour or a mixture of bright pastels. Each member of the company sits on one of these chairs when not involved in a sketch, in full view of the audience. The playing area front stage will be lit boldly, the rear areas in semi-darkness. It is imperative that the non-performers keep perfectly still and disciplined when not involved in a sketch. Each member of the company will have their personal props on, hanging from or under their chair.

The Presentation
Although *First Time* is a whole, each part is like a sketch from a revue and should be played in that style. For maximum effect the very short lines should be delivered with care but the cueing must be very sharp indeed for best comic effect.

At the beginning and end of each sketch there is a short strobe or freezelite effect when all the actors change their costumes, collect props and move any stage furniture into position. The strobe effect is accompanied by the "First Time" theme which will be found in the score. The whole effect should be of watching a silent film—actors moving at colossal speed. Even those actors who have no specific task to perform should invent some ad lib movement so that the whole stage is alive with business.

When the freezelite stops, the company will be in a freeze, holding the starting positions of the sketch. These positions are described at the beginning of each sketch. The more exaggerated and funny the starting positions, the more it adds to the general comedy. The lights come up on this freeze but the sketch does not start until the actors hear the sound effect single tone. After this, both sound and action commence.

The Music
See the composer's notes in the score.

The Costumes
The company may wear a simple basic costume on to which other costumes and props are added. This might be black leotards and black T-shirts or professionally made colourful costumes that blend with the overall concept. The costume changes must be done very quickly—keep the costume very simple but clear. Ensure where there are complications of change that Velcro is used to ensure rapid stripping of the costume. The simpler, the funnier. If you have any large costume you wish to incorporate e.g. the judge, then hang these costumes in the wings or off the playing area where a dresser can be deployed. Directors can tell their company to find their own costumes once they have cast. Very often this improvisational approach can produce some real surprises! Sometimes just a hat, a coat and a prop is sufficient to establish the character.

The Characters
The company play all the parts. These will have to be divided very carefully by the director and balanced to allow plenty of time for costume and furniture changes. **Marvin** can play only his own role but the others can be utilized throughout the show. Whenever parts become established such as **Julie** and **Marvin**'s mates at school, use the same actors each time to ensure continuity. There are moments in the show when very real sensitivity is required and the actors must be alert to these subtle changes. It is not *all* played for laughs. By the end, **Marvin** should be taken very seriously.

FIRST HALF*

The House Lights go down. The "First Time" theme is played increasing in volume as the Lights slowly come up

The Company walk into their places by their individual chairs. They stand facing the audience in semi-darkness

The Lights come up. The music stops to reveal Paul and Sally (about to be Marvin's Mum and Dad) and the Company in set positions

Song: First Time

Paul \
Sally / There's no cure for the pain
We endure each day we train,
For the part that our hearts
Will play in each new game,
Though we smile and we frown
We will always get let down.
The first time is always hard
You always feel a clown.

Company We are born to be involved in,
We could change the world—
We could solve the problems,
Every boy and girl.

Paul \
Sally / Leaving school, acting cool
There's no comfort for the fool.
You must laugh on the path,
You learn and break the rules.
From first fag you will brag
But there's bound to be a snag.
The first time is always hard
These days can be a drag.

Company We are born to be involved in,
We could change the world—
We could solve the problems,
Every boy and girl
Don't despair now you're here,
Don't try to skip by.
You are the one that can make it
The very First Time.

Strobe/freezelite for ten seconds accompanied by the theme

---

*N.B. Paragraph 3 on page ii of this Acting Edition regarding photocopying and video-recording should be carefully read.

Sketch: First Child

The strobe/freezelite stops and the Lights come up to reveal a queue at a bus stop. An asthmatic Old Man heads the queue, followed by a Business Man, a Trendy Lefty Lady, the husband Paul, the wife Sally who is very pregnant and finally Mrs P., an office cleaner. They are standing in a group freeze

A single tone. The freeze is broken and action/sound commences. Note: This sketch should get increasingly frenetic

Paul (*to his wife*) OK?
Sally Fine.
Paul Sure?
Sally Yes.

Pause

Mrs P. Going to the hospital?
Paul Yes. (*After a slight pause*) My wife's going to have a baby.

A slight pause

Mrs P. My mother had a baby.
Business Man We've only got your word for that.

Pause

   Probably on strike.
Sally Pardon?
Business Man Bus. Probably on strike.
Sally (*worried*) Paul.
Paul Don't worry. It'll be here.
Business Man Country's rife with strikes.
Mrs P. (*looking at Sally*) How long?
Paul Just under nine months.

A slight pause

Mrs P. Due any minute then.
Sally (*more worried*) Paul.
Paul Keep calm, Sally. There's no need to worry.
Mrs P. He's right, love. No need to panic. Let it all happen naturally.
Paul (*comforting*) You see, darling.
Mrs P. Otherwise it could end up deformed.
Sally Paul!!!
Business Man This is scandalous. Fifteen minutes late.
Lady It's always the same.
Business Man Don't I know it.
Lady You try to support the local transport, help them to keep the routes open and they don't even turn up. It's scandalous.
Business Man Probably on strike.
Lady Lightning strike.

First Time

Business Man Quite. The whole country's on strike in my opinion. Buses, miners. (*After a slight pause*) Nurses——

They all turn and look at Sally. Paul comforts her

——the whole National Health Service is falling to pieces.
Lady The government.
Business Man And the government, they're falling to pieces.

Pause

Old Man (*wheezing*) Here—it—comes.

They all lean out in the road to get a good view of the approaching bus

Business Man Damn! It's turned off.
Lady At least they're moving.

A slight pause

Sally Paul. I can feel stirrings.
Paul No.
Sally Yes.
Paul You just imagined it.
Sally I didn't.
Paul Yes.
Sally I should know, damn it!
Paul All right. Keep calm.

The rest of the queue are looking at the tiff. The couple smile at everyone and make it up

Old Man (*wheezing heavily now*) Here—it—comes.

They all lean out again. A slight pause. Eyes return to the front. It's turned off. Nothing to be said. Resignation

Mrs P. Wotcher want? Boy or a girl?
Sally (*perking up*) I don't mind. I'd prefer a boy, but I don't really mind.
Mrs P. I'd prefer a girl.
Sally Oh?
Mrs P. (*doom-laden*) Girls live longer than boys.
Sally (*panicky*) Paul!
Paul All right. Please don't. You're upsetting my wife.
Mrs P. Sorry.
Paul Thank you.
Mrs P. Only trying to be friendly.
Old Man (*excited*) Here—it——(*He realizes he's made a mistake*)

They all glare at him

Another Man and Woman join the queue

Sally (*panic increasing*) It's not coming.
Paul Of course it's coming.

Sally When?
Paul Soon. It'll be here soon.
Man Huh! What an optimist.

A slight pause. Suddenly Sally twitches and looks out front

Sally (*whispering*) Paul. (*She is rigid*) Paul.
Paul Yes darling?
Sally It's coming.
Paul Oh good. (*He looks up the road*) I told you it wouldn't be long.
Sally It's coming Paul, it's coming.
Paul Where darling? I can't see it.
Sally The baby Paul. The baby's coming.
Paul What!

Sally screams and clutches her stomach

Man What is it?
Paul (*confused panic*) My baby's going to have a wife.
Sally Oh God!

Paul helps her to the ground

Man A baby?

Everyone in the queue exits rapidly. They don't want to know

Sally Paul.
Paul Don't panic. Keep calm. (*Shouting after the disappearing queue*) Can someone call an ambulance? Please don't go. I don't know what to do. (*He goes to follow them*)
Sally Paul!

He returns to her side

Paul Yes dear. I'll get ... (*He starts to go*)
Sally Don't leave me.
Paul (*coming back*) Right.
Sally Get help.
Paul Right. (*He starts to go*)
Sally But don't leave me.

He comes back

Two Old Spinsters enter. They look like Hinge and Bracket

Paul Can you help me? My wife's going to have a baby.
Emily Oh super.
Violet Boy or girl? Shouldn't she be in hospital or something?
Sally (*with feeling*) Yes.
Emily I'll go for an ambulance.
Violet There's a little phone box further on.
Paul Thank you.
Emily Oh. I've just remembered, Violet. There's one back there as well.

Violet Well, which one is the nearer, Emily? The one back there or the one further on.
Emily The one back there.
Violet Are you sure?
Emily Positive! (*A slight pause*) I think.
Violet It seemed quite a long way back to me.
Paul Please hurry.
Emily We're just trying to work out which one is the nearest, young man. Don't waste time do we, Violet?
Violet Certainly not. I'll go to the one further on and take a chance.
Emily Right.
Violet It'll be best if Emily stays.
Paul Why?
Violet She's got her post-natal badge.
Sally (*moaning*) Oh God.
Paul Please hurry.
Violet I'm off.

Violet exits

Emily Isn't this exciting. I've never seen a baby born in the street before.
Paul Nor have I.
Emily I was born in the toilet you know.
Paul Really?
Emily Yes. The door handle broke off while my mother was in there.

She laughs and nearly has heart failure. Paul helps her to recover

Paul How interesting.
Sally (*interrupting*) Paul—I think ...
Paul Don't worry.
Emily Violet's gone to the phone box.
Sally I think ...
Paul They'll soon be here.
Sally I think ... it's passed.
Paul Passed?

Violet returns

Are you sure?
Emily It's all right. It's passed.
Violet The phone box wasn't working.
Sally I think it's ...
Paul Do you want to sit up?
Sally Yes. (*She sits up*) No! (*She goes straight down again*)
Paul Which?
Sally Yes.

He helps her to sit up

No! It's coming again! (*She lies back down*)

Emily Quick, Violet.
Violet I'm off.

Violet exits in the wrong direction

Sally (*moaning*) Oh.
Paul I don't know what to do.

A Policeman and Policewoman enter

Policeman What's going on here?
Paul I'm going to have a baby.
Policeman You trying to be funny sir?
Paul (*confused*) I mean my baby's going to have a wife—baby. Please help.
Policeman Are you sure, madam?
Sally (*moaning*) Oh.
Policeman Ah.

Violet enters

Violet Sorry. Wrong way.

Violet exits in the correct direction

Policeman How long is she?
Paul About five foot three. (*He watches Violet toddle off*)
Policeman No sir. Not her. How long is your wife in time?
Paul Oh ... nine months.
Policeman (*inspiration*) Then ... it could be due any minute.
Paul (*long-suffering*) Yes. Like now.
Policewoman Shall I deal with this, Frank. My role is more of a community relations brief than yours.
Policeman Over to you, Sandra.
Policewoman Can you hear me madam?
Sally (*groaning*) Oh.
Policewoman Now just keep calm and we'll do the rest.
Policeman Shall I loosen her clothing?

They all stare at him as if he's a dirty old man

A bit?
Policewoman That won't be necessary, Frank.
Policeman Very well, Sandra.

The sound of a bus approaching is heard

All the people in the queue suddenly appear from various hiding points on the set and chase after the rapidly departing bus

Paul It's a bus!
Policeman Very good sir. Bit of a spotter are we?

Bus and queue have now vanished as Violet enters

Violet The one back there's not working either.

First Time

Sally Oh Paul. Paul.
Paul (*panic*) Oh God. God.
Policewoman Right. Now she must be kept warm——

They all crowd round her

—but she must have air——

They all breathe on her

—I mean coats and things to keep her warm.

They all start to take off warming clothes and place them on or around Sally

Violet I just couldn't get through to the hospital.
Policeman Don't worry madam. We'll do that . . . (*He takes out a two-way radio*) Six-six-six . . . (*he realizes that he is holding it upside down, turns it the right way up and pulls out the aerial*) . . . nine, nine, nine. CID? Sid, send an ambulance to the High Street. Over and up.
Sally Wait a minute.
Paul Don't worry, Sally.
Sally But I——
Policewoman Don't worry madam. Your husband's right. Everything is under control.
Sally But I think it's all right.
Policewoman Sure?
Paul Remember what happened last time?
Sally No. I'm sure.

Sally sits up. The Policeman returns to the group

Policeman The ambulance is on its way.
Policewoman We don't need it.
Policeman (*hurt*) I see.
Sally It's passed.

The Policeman takes out his radio again

Paul Are you absolutely certain?
Policeman Cancel that ambulance, Sid.
Sally Yes . . . No!
Policeman (*into the radio*) Hang on.
Sally (*feeling her stomach*) Yes.
Policeman Cancel that—
Sally (*sudden clutch*) No!
Policeman Make up your mind love.
Sally I don't know. Oooooh! (*She falls back.* It's for real)
Policeman (*panic, as he fumbles and shakes with nerves*) Get that ambulance here.

A Man (Docker) enters with a dark overcoat and bag

Docker Can I help at all?
Policewoman What are you?

The Man indistinctly says a word that sounds like "doctor"

    Then you certainly can.
Paul My wife's going to have a baby.
Docker Which one's your wife?
Paul Her, down there.
Docker Afternoon.
Policewoman We've called for an ambulance.
Docker Oh good.
Violet We've been keeping her warm.
Sally Oooooh.

They all crowd round except the Docker who looks at his watch and starts to walk off

Policewoman Where are you going?
Docker To work.
Policewoman But shouldn't you help here?
Docker There's not much I can do.
Paul You're a doctor!
Docker Docker! I said I'm a docker! (*He opens his coat to reveal a grease-stained vest and overalls*)
Policeman Clear off! You interfering little twit.
Docker I only asked if I could help.
Policeman Go on clear off — before I call a policeman.

The Docker exits

Sally (*urgently now*) Oooooh.

They all crowd round again

Policewoman Don't worry madam.
Paul What are you going to do?
Violet Emily, you should be able to do something.
Emily No. I only know what to do afterwards.
Policeman Look, the ambulance should be here soon.
Paul Sally. Hang on.
Policewoman Keep her warm.

They close in

    But don't suffocate her.

They all back off. The group now have their backs to the audience so that only the pregnant Sally can see the passers-by

Policeman The ambulance is definitely on its way.
Emily I don't think there was a badge for pre-natal.
Policewoman Oh God. I feel faint.
Policeman Steady Sandra. Hold on. Community relations and all that.
Violet I think she's going to pass out.
Sally OOOOOOH!

First Time

Paul Heavens! It's coming. She's going to have it.
Emily Push.
Policeman Altogether now. Push!
Violet Push.
Policewoman Oh God. I feel terrible.
All (*continuous, ad lib*) Push ... That's the way ... Be brave darling ... Push ... Don't you push me ...

During this sequence a long line of people pass by, all chatting as if going for a lunch-break—Nurses, St John's Ambulance Men, Surgeons, Doctors, Matrons, etc. Sally can see them all and tries to draw the attention of the well-meaning group to them. They are so busy trying to do the right thing that they are oblivious of her dilemma. Suddenly a baby cries. Silence. They all look out front

All (*out front—half of the group*) It's a boy!
(*the other half simultaneously*) It's a girl!

They all look back at the baby

(*Again confused and together*) It's a boy/It's a girl!

They all look back again, then at each other, smile and give knowing laughs and say

It's a **BABY**!!!

Sally and Paul move DR *with their new baby*

Song: Baby

Sally
Paul
A baby is a bundle of joy—
A baby is a girl or a boy.
But there's more to it we know,
Than watching Baby grow.

Babies they need loving,
Babies must be warm.
Parents there to guide them,
Watch them taking form.
It needs us now
To show it how
To make its way through life.

Three Mothers as a backing group enter DL. *They each carry a baby wrapped in blankets*

Three Mothers It'll wake you up at half-past four,
Needing feeding and plenty more.
You won't sleep 'til the crack of dawn,
By then you'll wish it hadn't been born.

During this last line all the Company Girls enter, carrying babies

Company Cry, cry, cry, cry.
Wet, wet, wet, wet,
Howl, howl, howl, howl,
Scream, scream, scream, scream.

The Three Mothers exit

The Company Girls stay on stage in a group freeze

Sally } Surely now, that can't be all
Paul } For more than that, it is ours.
Doesn't matter what you say
You will not put us off
A baby's what we wanted
And a baby's what we've got.
It seems a shame
That you won't change your mind
About this fact.

During this last line, the Three Mothers return DL *carrying two or three babies. One has a papoose on her back. During the following chorus the Company Girls play "pass the parcel" and the Company Men enter, pushing prams and pushchairs*

Mothers } It'll scream and holler, night and day,
Girls   } Your hands will shake
And your brain'll give way.
Only twenty but you're looking old,
Your eyes are heavy
And you're feeling the cold.
Three Mothers Pain, pain, pain, pain.
Company Girls Throb, Throb, Throb, Throb.
Company Men   Mum, Mum, Mum, Mum.
All   Scream, scream, scream, scream.

Babies are attacked and chucked about in a very funny fashion during the last two lines

Scream, scream, scream, scream.
Scream, scream, scream, scream.
Sally Surely now, that can't be all.
Paul   For more than that
It's ...

To fortissimo introduction Marvin is revealed in a tight spot. Marvin wears national health glasses, the lenses held together with elastoplast. He is scabby at the knees, wears short trousers, is short-sighted, squints and has a finger up his nose

... MARVIN!

Paul (*speaking*) Marvin!
Sally (*speaking*) Dirty boy!

First Time

Paul (*speaking*) Pull it out!

Marvin extracts his finger and wipes it on his trousers

All (*in total disgust*) Eeeeeeaaaaarrrrrrch!

Strobe/freezelite as the Company change for the next scene accompanied by the theme

Sketch: First Fag

The strobe/freezelite stops and the Lights come up to reveal a playground scene. It is the lunch break in a mixed comprehensive. The frozen group of players are Sid, a first-year coward and bully, Tom his sidekick and Marvin who is maturing somewhat slowly. Facing them are three first-year girls; June, Brenda and Gloria. The girls are tougher than Sid and any of his mates. The school is ruled by Nutty Norman of the fifth year, Nutty Norman's gang and Mr Turner, a teacher—in that order. A playground handbell is ringing with off-stage noises of kids messing about

Notes: The chases across the stage should be fast, furious and funny. The characters can be dressed as modern day pupils but the sketch is much funnier if they are dressed like schoolchildren in a kid's comic complete with school caps, short trousers (long trousers rolled up) school ties askew, rumpled shirts, scabby knees and socks round the ankles. The girls look like St Trinian hoydens while Nutty and his entourage dress in a way that suggests a flagrant disregard for school rules and correct school dress

Sid What year are you girls in?
June First year.
Sid Oh yeah.
Marvin (*weedy*) So are we.
Sid You don't look like first years to me.
Brenda Well, we are.
Marvin Fancy a fag?
Sid All right Marvin I'll handle this.
June You their leader?
Tom (*naïvely*) No. Milk monitor.

The girls laugh at them

June (*sneering*) Milk monitor?
Sid And leader.
Tom Oh yeah—that an' all.
Brenda How big's your gang?
Tom Just us——
Sid (*interrupting*) Here at the moment. The rest have gone on the nature trip.
June Why ain't you wiv' em?
Sid (*hard*) Not allowed.
Tom No.

Sid What did Mr Turner call us, Tom?
Tom (*tough*) Trouble-makers.
Sid (*menacing*) Yeah, that's right. Trouble-makers.
Marvin And scum.
Sid Yer all right, Marvin.
Marvin And big Jessies.
Tom Marvin! Just leave it out. OK?
Gloria (*contemptuous*) What sort of trouble d'you make then?
Sid (*thrown momentarily*) Eh?
Gloria (*slowly*) What sort of trouble do you cause?

A slight pause

Sid All sorts.
Gloria Oh yeah? Well my brother murdered an old lady of ninety-three.

A slight pause

Marvin Sid smashed a thrush's egg.

Sid and Tom glare at Marvin

Tom Well, it was quite a big one.
Marvin I killed a spider yesterday ... on my own.
Gloria (*sneering*) You ain't 'ard.
Sid Didn't say we were, did we?
Tom No. Didn't say we were.

The girls turn their backs on the boys—unimpressed

Sid (*desperate*) We robbed a bank.
Marvin No we didn't.
Sid (*through his teeth*) Yes we did.
Marvin When?
Sid Didn't we Tom?
Tom Yeah.
Marvin Well, I can't remember.
Sid That's 'cos you weren't there.

They glare at him

Tom Yeah, I remember now, Marvin. You were out shoppin' wiv your mum.
Marvin Saturday afternoon?
Tom Yeah.
Gloria Banks aren't open on Saturday afternoons.
Sid This one was ... (*after a slight pause*) ... it was late-day closing.
Brenda There's no such thing.
Sid Yes there is.
Marvin No there ain't.
Tom Marvin—I'll thump you in a minute.

He stamps on his foot. Marvin is speechless with pain

First Time

June (*querulous*) You as hard as Nutty Norman?
Sid What, in the fifth year?
June Yeah.
Sid Course I am, ain't I ...?

Silence. Sid looks at Tom and Marvin for vocal support

Ain't I?
Tom ⎫
Marvin ⎭ (*together*) Oh yeah!!
Brenda Think you could do 'im?
Sid (*confused*) Do 'im what?
June Do 'im in.
Sid No trouble.
Gloria Prove it.
Sid I would if he was here.
Gloria Good. 'Cos he's coming now.

They spin round, terrified, but nobody's there

Sid Very funny.
Tom Made my heart stop.
Sid He don't scare me.
Marvin He does me.
Tom (*without thinking*) And me ...

Sid glares at Tom

A little bit.
Sid I beat 'im up the other day.
Gloria Oh yeah?
Sid Weren't nothing to it.

Nutty Norman and his mates enter

He was a pushover.
Brenda Who was?
Sid Who was what?
Brenda Who was a pushover?
Sid Nutty Norman.

Nutty is alerted by the mention of his name and slowly sidles over in Sid's direction. The girls giggle as Sid signs his own death warrant. Tom and Marvin are aghast at the approaching danger and stand open-mouthed

(*Aside to Tom*) I think they're impressed.
Tom (*trying to warn Sid*) Sid.
Sid Leave it to me, Tom.
Tom Sid!
Sid What are you girls doin' tonight?
Gloria What do you think of him?
Sid Who?
Gloria Norman.

Sid He's a prat.
Tom Sid!!
Brenda You must be hard if you beat up Nutty Norman on your own.

Tom and Marvin have edged round to the other side with the girls. Norman has moved up behind the oblivious Sid

Sid Told you I was. 'Ere where are you two goin'?
Tom Er ... well, Sid.
Marvin To get help.
Sid For who?

Norman grabs Sid, spins him round, fist raised

Not my face! Not my face!

Mr Turner, the teacher, enters R

Turner Norman! I want a word with you!
Sid Turner wants to see you.
Turner Now!

Norman reluctantly releases Sid and exits behind Turner followed by his gang

Sid See.
Marvin Now you're for it.
June Can we watch?
Sid What?
June When he smashes your face in after school.
Gloria June likes blood.
Sid Well she ought to go out with Marvin. He's a little bleeder.

Sid and Tom laugh coarsely

June (*quite taken with him*) Your name Marvin?
Marvin Yeah. Fancy a fag?
June Why? you got some?
Marvin Yeah. (*He takes out a huge packet*)
Brenda Bet you can't smoke.
Tom He can.
Sid Never mind the smoking. What about tonight?
Marvin (*spotting Norman returning*) Nutty Norman!
Sid Oh blimey!

Sid exits at high speed hounded by Nutty Norman and his gang hurling abuse after Sid and making it clear what they will do to his body when they catch him

Gloria (*to Marvin*) Go on then. Let's see you.

Marvin takes out a fag and lights it in a very flashy manner, but smokes it very inexpertly

June (*to Tom*) Where'd he learn to do that?

First Time

Tom From the anti-smoking video.
Marvin (*to June*) Wanna go?
June All right. (*She takes a drag, coughs and splutters*)
Brenda Careful June, you might get lung cancer.
Tom Not just from one puff.
Brenda No?
Tom No ... it takes at least three.
Gloria How do you know?
Tom Marvin worked it out on his home computer——

Marvin has taken another huge drag

—didn't you Marve?
Marvin Yeah. Anyone else?

Sid flashes past upstage followed by Norman and the screaming hordes. Norman says nothing as he leads the band but they shout things like "Nut 'im Norman", "Do 'im over" and "Chew 'is ear off"

Sid (*screaming it out as he passes*) I'll be in the girls' toilets.
Tom (*noticing Marvin is pale*) You all right Marvin?
Marvin I feel funny.
Brenda He's got lung cancer.
Marvin No. It's not the same feeling as lung cancer.
Tom No?
Marvin No. It's a different kind of feeling. A "funny" feeling.
Gloria Let's 'ave a look.

Gloria takes Marvin's fag

Marvin I feel funny.
Gloria (*inspecting the fag*) Looks all right.

Marvin goes wobbly at the knees

Tom Don't let Turner see him.
Brenda Hold him up.

Tom and June support the collapsing Marvin

Gloria There's a piece of grass on it—but that's all.
Brenda Grass?
Gloria Yeah.
Brenda That's a drug.
Gloria What is?
Brenda Grass. When you smoke it.
Gloria Is it?
Marvin I feel terrible.
Brenda My brother told me.
Marvin (*groaning*) Ooooooh!
Tom Don't worry Marvin, we've got you.
Marvin I feel sick!

Tom and June immediately drop him

Gloria He's on drugs.

Marvin crawls away to DR

Brenda He'll go on a trip.
Tom He's gone already.
June Grab him.

Sid enters. He's escaped

Sid A lot of help you two were.
Tom Marvin's on drugs.
Sid What for? Doctor's orders?
Tom It's serious, Sid.
Brenda He's been smoking grass.
Sid So?
Gloria He's tougher than you are.
Sid Who says?
Gloria I do. When Nutty Norman came over you went all white.
Sid No I didn't.
Gloria Yes you did.
Sid I've been ill.
Marvin (*still on his knees*) I feel funny.
Sid How about comin' down to the tennis courts?
June What about your mate?
Sid (*looking down at Marvin*) Leave him here.
Brenda Not much of a mate are you?
Sid He's a prat.
Marvin I heard that.

Note: the next three lines can be omitted at the Director's discretion

Sid You would. You've got ears like Noddy.
Tom Noddy didn't have Big Ears.
Sid No. But not through lack of trying.

A slight pause

Come on. What about it? We can have a game of doubles.
Gloria Who?
Sid Tom and Brenda and you and me.
Brenda What about June?
Sid She can look after Marvin.
Brenda Charming.
June (*having taken a shine to the helpless Marvin*) I don't mind.
Gloria What if there's someone on the courts?
Sid (*really tough*) If there is, I'll kick 'em off. Come on.

Sid exits towards the tennis courts

Gloria See you later, June.
Tom Cheerio Marvin.
Sid (*shouting; off*) Oi! Get off them courts, you faggots!

First Time

Gloria, Brenda and Tom exit towards the courts

June You all right?
Marvin Yeah. Not too bad.
June Sure?
Marvin Must've been the sun.
June (*putting a fag under Marvin's nose*) Want another?
Marvin (*going green*) Not just yet.
June Why?

A burst of murderous noise as Sid flees across the stage with Tom, Brenda and Gloria. In hot pursuit are Norman and his gang. They are hurling tennis balls at them and waving rackets menacingly. They exit and there is complete silence

Marvin I'm trying to give 'em up.

The Company return at pace and take up positions during the introductory bars of the next song. Norman's gang use rackets as guitars in the choreography of the number

Song: Can You Remember? (*Aggresso fortissimo*)

Boys	Can you remember the first time you had a fag?
Girls	Can you remember? Can you remember?
Boys	Can you remember the first time you took a drag?
Girls	Can you remember? Can you remember?
	Was it in the playground bog?
	Did you feel sick as a dog?
All	Can you remember? Can you remember?
	What a feeling
	Was you dreaming.
	Can you remember?
Girls	Can you remember the first time you bought a bra?
Boys	Can you remember? Can you remember?
Girls	Can you remember you moved like a movie star?
Boys	Can you remember? Can you remember?
Girls	Thirty "A" cup that didn't fit,
	Bits fell out so you felt a—twit.
All	Can you remember? Can you remember?
	Taking shape,
	Using all the sticky tape
	Can you remember?
	Did you guess?
	It was your first time.
Boys	Can you remember the first time you pulled a bird?
Girls	Can you remember? Can you remember?
Boys	Tellin' her that you would not breathe a word.

Girls	Can you remember? Can you remember?
Boys	Stood you up on your very first date,
	Now she's goin' out with yer closest mate.
All	Can you remember? Can you remember?
	Acted cool,
	Must have looked a fool—
	Can you remember?
	Can you remember the first time you got drunk?
Girls	Can you remember? Can you remember?
All	Stumblin' around and you thought your head 'ad shrunk
Girls	Can you remember? Can you remember?
All	In the loo with yer clothes still on,
	Watching the space where yer money had gone.
	Can you remember? Can you remember?
	What a pain,
	Wages down the drain
	Can you remember?
	Did you guess
	It was your First Time
	Can you remember? Can you remember?
	Can you remember? Right!

Strobe/freezelite comes on for not more than ten seconds as the Company change for the next scene. Link theme tune "First Time"

Sketch: First Job

The stobe/freezelite stops and the Lights come up to reveal Marvin seated on a small wooden bench. L *There is a display board behind him on which is pinned "career griff"—"Join the Army", "It's a Man's Life" and "A Career with Barclays means Security" etc. He is waiting to enter the Careers Officer's office* L. *The Careers Officer is seated at a small table. Office bric-a-brac as required. Doreen is provocatively placing a cup of tea on the table*

Single tone. The freeze is broken. Action and sound start

> *Doreen puts down the cup and exits*

Officer (*going to an imaginary door as Doreen exits in the opposite direction*) Marvin? Come in please.
Marvin Right.
Officer Sit down.
Marvin Thanks.
Officer Now Marvin. There are a few routine questions and then we'll see if we can find you a niche in life.

Marvin is seated. The Officer looks at a paper then looks up. He removes his glasses

> Now Marvin, have you ever had a job before?

First Time

Marvin (*joking*) Well, I had a job getting up this morning.
Officer (*not given to humour*) Pardon?
Marvin (*removing the grin from his face*) No.
Officer Good. Would you like some tea?
Marvin Yes please.
Officer (*into the intercom*) Doreen. Tea please. (*To Marvin*) Now to work. (*He picks up a pen*) Right. Marvin Tadler.
Marvin What?
Officer Your name is Marvin Tadler?
Marvin Yes.
Officer English?
Marvin (*thinking for a moment*) Yes.
Officer No Marvin. The subject "English". How did you do?
Marvin Not bad.
Officer Maths?
Marvin Adding up and taking away was all right but algebra and multiplication baffled me.
Officer Too difficult eh?
Marvin No. I couldn't spell 'em.
Officer Geography?
Marvin (*thinking hard*) G ... E ... O ... G ... R—— (*He is interrupted by Doreen's entrance*)

Doreen enters with a cup of tea. She wiggles in and places the cup seductively on the table, then exits. Her entrance and exit are accompanied by music similar to "The Stripper"

Marvin watches her open-mouthed. He has never seen anything quite as gorgeous as Doreen

Officer OK. Let's take the academic side as read, shall we?
Marvin (*stupified by the retreating vision*) Is that your secretary?
Officer (*impatient*) Yes. Now is there any particular job you would like?
Marvin Yes. (*He looks at the Officer*) Yours.
Officer Seriously.
Marvin Seriously.
Officer What about insurance? (*He picks up a pamphlet*)
Marvin I can look after meself, thanks.
Officer (*exasperated*) I mean a job in insurance.
Marvin What's the money like?
Officer How much do you expect?
Marvin More than you'd get on a paper round.
Officer How much do you get on a paper round?
Marvin Not as much as you'd expect.
Officer Marvin!
Marvin I once drove a milk float.
Officer This isn't getting us very far.
Marvin That's what I said.
Officer (*sharp and annoyed*) Marvin! (*He stands*) What does your father do?

Marvin When?
Officer During the day.
Marvin He goes to work.
Officer (*he's talking to an idiot*) What—sort—of—work.
Marvin I'm not sure. He's a doctor of some kind, doing research into why people tell lies.
Officer I see. (*He sit and writes this down*)
Marvin Well, that's what he tells us.

The Officer stops, slams down his pen and rips off his glasses

Officer I am supposed to be helping you find a job!
Marvin I know. And you're not doing very well. But don't blame yourself.

The Officer has nearly had enough. He switches on the intercom

Officer Doreen. Would you please bring in some aspirin.
Marvin (*sympathetically*) I'm just difficult to place.

Doreen enters with a glass of water and aspirin—walk and music as before—then exits

Marvin It's probably her that's given you the headache.

The Officer takes the aspirin

Can't be easy to concentrate with her around.

A slight pause

Officer (*calmed*) Now, let's start again shall we?
Marvin Let's.
Officer Now. Do you want a career?
Marvin I'd rather have a job.
Officer Now we're getting somewhere.
Marvin Good.
Officer In what?
Marvin What?
Officer What would you like a job in? Where would you like to work? What do you want to do when—you—leave—school?

Silence. A slight pause. The Officer glares

Marvin What. For a living?
Officer (*tight-lipped*) Yes.

Pause

Marvin Hadn't really thought about it.
Officer (*through his teeth*) Well. Think—about—it—now.

A slight pause

Marvin (*confidentially*) How much does Bobby Crush get?
Officer (*bemused*) I haven't the faintest idea.
Marvin I see.

First Time

Officer Do you play the piano?
Marvin No.
Officer Have you got a piano?
Marvin No.
Officer Then how the hell do you think you're going to earn your living as a PIANIST!!!
Marvin Pianist? I thought he was a wrestler!

The Officer stands up. He is livid

Officer That's it!
Marvin (*elated*) You really think I could be a wrestler then?
Officer (*hands on the desk, leaning slowly towards Marvin*) I think you'd better get out of this office before I do something we'll both regret. But you more than me.

The Officer now has his face looking straight into Marvin's eyes, inches away

Marvin (*unflinching, speaking very softly*) What about an actor?

Pause. Neither moves a muscle

Officer Actor?
Marvin (*softly*) I wouldn't mind being an actor.
Officer (*acidic*) Have you any acting experience?
Marvin Yes. I was in the school play.
Officer Good. (*He slowly starts to sit in his chair*)
Marvin Shakespeare. *The Merry Wives of Waterford.*

The Officer pauses in his descent after this remark

Officer So you like acting, eh Marvin?
Marvin (*Long John Silver*) "Oooo Arrrr Jim lad".
Officer And you'd like to give it a try?
Marvin (*declaiming*) "To be or not to be".
Officer Tread the boards.
Marvin (*declaiming*) "The Bells!! The Bells!!"
Officer It's not as glamorous as you think, Marvin.
Marvin (*declaiming*) "A horse, a horse, my Lambretta for a horse".
Officer Listen! I said it's not quite a glamorous as you think, Marvin.
Marvin Isn't it?
Officer No. In fact it can be pretty demanding.
Marvin Can it?
Officer Yes. A very close friend of mine went into the acting profession.
Marvin What happened to him?
Officer Well he went for the part of Araham Lincoln in a West End production. He was very good. He auditioned and got the part. For six weeks he worked very hard at the character. He spoke like him, walked like him and even looked like him. And do you know what happened after the first night, Marvin?
Marvin No.
Officer He was assassinated.

A slight pause. The Officer moves round the desk

But if you'd like to come with me Marvin, I have a colleague who has influential connections with our local rep company and he might be able to pull a few strings.

The Officer guides Marvin to the imaginary door

But I must warn you, Marvin, an actor's life is by no means a bed of pansies.

Marvin You mean roses.
Officer I know what I mean.

Black-out. They exit

The strobe/freezelite comes on for not more than ten seconds as the Company change for the backstage sequence. Link theme tune "First Time"

Sketch: First Night

The strobe/freezelite stops and the Lights come up to reveal backstage before a production of "Who Knows". Betty sits at a table R. She is putting on make-up. She is bossy and thinks she's the star. Sandra is standing C. She is unflappable and efficient. Rene collecting props is the Stage Manager—incapable of making a decision without consulting the director Ray. Ray is offstage ready to welcome local dignitaries. Also off are Debbie—dizzy and vain; Dora—a hypochondriac, disorganized and a danger to all around her; and Marvin

There is a second table LC at which Sandra and Debbie will make up. Further L is Dora's table covered in bottles and tablets. UC is a paper screen on which is painted framed picture

Single tone. The freeze is broken. Action and sound start

Rene Twenty minutes to curtain up.

Rene sweeps through and off

Betty That chair that's on the right.
Sandra (*putting on a dress*) Stage right?
Betty Pardon?
Sandra Stage right?
Betty How do you mean?
Sandra Do you mean stage right?
Betty Oh I can never remember which is which.
Sandra It's easy. Stage right is on the left.
Betty Right.
Sandra Left!
Betty Right or left, it's in the way.
Sandra So?
Betty Perhaps you can move it before I come on.

Rene enters

Rene (*sweeping through*) I'm Stage Manager.
Betty Well, you move it.
Rene I'll have to check it out with Ray.

Rene exits

Betty You can check it with the Archbishop of Canterbury for all I care—just as long as the chair's moved.

Debbie enters. She is dizzy and a bit of a wreck

Sandra Debbie. Hi!

Rene enters

Rene You're late.
Debbie Sorry. Babysitter.
Rene I'll let Ray know that you're here.

Rene exits

Debbie moves to the table and plonks herself down next to Sandra who has started to do her face

Sandra You've only got five minutes.
Debbie Don't you start. It's bad enough with Barbara Woodhouse out there.

Dora enters. She is slow and disorganized

Dora I feel faint. (*She lumbers to the medicine table*)
Debbie (*panicky*) Where's my costume?
Sandra You're sitting on it.
Debbie Oh yeah.

Rene sweeps in

Rene Betty, I've just realized I can't move that chair. I'm doing the coffee.
Betty Well somebody's got to move it.
Dora What chair?
Sandra The chair on the left.
Betty Right.
Sandra Stage right.
Betty The audience's left.
Rene So somebody else will have to move it.
Betty If that chair is not moved before I enter I shall hurl it into the front row.

Rene exits in disgust

Sandra Temper. Temper.

Pat enters with flowers. He's a "nice" boy

Pat Flowers for the star.
Betty (*pleased*) Oh.

Pat Here you are Debbie.
Betty (*not so pleased*) Oh.
Debbie For me? Oooo they're lovely.
Pat Who are they from?
Debbie (*looking at the card*) It doesn't say.
Pat Secret admirer. Lucky old you.

Dora sneezes. Pat puts the flowers in a vase near Dora. Dora sneezes again

Bless you.
Dora I'm allergic to flowers.
Sandra You would be.
Pat Especially when they're somebody else's.
Betty How's it going to be out there?
Pat Out front? Filling up nicely. Problems in the men's dressing rooms though.
Sandra Marvin?
Pat Drunk.
Betty Marvellous.
Pat They're trying to sober him up now.
Betty He's hopeless. I don't know what he's doing in the company.
Debbie He'll be all right.
Betty It's all right for you. I've got to do the love scene in Act Three with him. He reeks like a brewery.
Dora D'ye think he'd like some Polos?
Pat I'll nip back there and give 'im the kiss of life.

Pat minces off. Rene enters

Rene Action Stations! Ray is coming backstage with the Mayor and guests.
Betty What?
Rene You heard.
Dora Anyone seen my hay fever tablets?
Debbie I'm not dressed.
Betty We haven't sorted out my chair.
Sandra You and your blinkin' chair. Whoever sits on it can move it.
Betty That's just it. Who does sit on it?
Rene (*to Betty*) You do!
Betty (*embarrassed*) Oh.

Rene exits

Marvin enters, drunk

Marvin Ladies may I have the pleasure——
Sandra Oh God ... No!
Marvin —of wishing you all the very very very best of luck on this our very very very first night and offer you all (*hic*) a good luck drink.
Dora He's drunk. (*She starts doing deep-breathing exercises*)
Marvin Betty, I love you.
Betty Marvin get off. Where are my Anadins?

First Time

Sandra Marvin get out of here.
Debbie (*holding up a bottle of tablets*) Are these them?
Sandra Marvin. Go!!

Rene enters, holding a chair

Rene Is this the chair that's causing all the trouble?
Marvin (*to Rene*) Have a drink, Rene. I think I love you.
Betty They're hay fever tablets.
Debbie They must be Dora's.
Betty Dora, have you got my Anadins?
Marvin Rene. You are the very very very most beautiful woman I've ever seen.
Rene Don't be stupid.
Marvin Rene, I love you.
Betty The bottle's half empty.
Marvin I think I love you.
Debbie Dora!

Dora collapses

She must've taken an overdose.
Rene Oh God.
Sandra She needs air.
Debbie Sit her up.
Rene Fan her.

Rene grabs the flowers and starts waving them over Dora

Marvin (*lurching across*) I'm a doctor.
Sandra You're pickled.
Marvin I'm a pickled doctor.
Debbie They're my flowers!
Marvin They're feautiful blowers.
Debbie Rene, let go. (*Pulling the flowers away*).
Sandra Betty, she needs water.
Marvin Dora, I love you.
Betty For God's sake, Marvin.

Debbie tears away the flowers and they scatter. Sandra throws water from the vase at Dora who collapses again so that Rene who is behind Dora gets a faceful. Betty pushes Marvin who falls into a chair which collapses. They are all screaming as Ray, Pat and the Mayor plus dignitaries enter

Ray Why don't you all——
Betty (*interrupting, whirling round*) Get stuffed! (*She realizes who it is*) Your Worship.

She curtsies and the others likewise

Ray The Mayor just wanted to ... wish you the best of luck.
Mayor (*oblivious to the chaos*) Don't want to panic you. See you're warming

up. Catch the flavour backstage you know, smell of the greasebag and all that. Break a leg.
Marvin (*lurching forward and embracing the Mayor*) Marry me!
Mayor Good God!
Betty bursts into tears and general chaos breaks out
 The Mayor beats a hasty retreat

Song: First Night Blues

All
First night blues got to hold on,
First night blues, when I go on,
First night blues got a hold on me.

Solo
Standing in the wings I feel
Everything is so unreal.
Curtains rise and then I steal the show.
Standing with the lights ablaze,
Every laugh that I can raise,
Helps me through that awkward stage you know.

Chorus
First night blues got a hold on
First night blues, when I go on
First night blues got a hold on me.

Solo
Mind goes blank and mouth goes dry,
Can't remember, don't know why.
Frozen stiff, I want to die, oh——
From the wings I hear them call,
Mumbling words that mean "B" all.
Marvin's entered through the wall, oh——

Marvin tumbles through the wall, bottle in hand
Chorus

Chorus
Set falls in on Marvin's head,
The body moves that should be dead.
Perhaps I should've stayed in bed, oh——
Finally the curtain's jammed,
Everybody starts to ham,
But I couldn't give a damn, oh——

Chorus

Chorus 1 Why do people want to go
   2 On to the stage and do a show
   3 Only they can really know, oh——
   4 Broke and homeless for no pay
   5 They keep working night and day,
   6 And all his friends are flipping/bloody gay—oh——

First Time

> First night blues, got to hold on
> First night blues, when I go on
> First night blues got a hold on me
> First night blues got to hold on
> First night blues, when I go on
> First night blues got a hold on
> Got a hold on, got a hold on
> Got a hold on
> Me!

Freeze

The Careers Officer enters

Officer Marvin.
Marvin Yes?
Officer I did warn you!
Marvin Yes.
Officer This is not the career for you Marvin. Get up.
Marvin Get up?
Officer Get out.
Marvin Get out?
Officer And grow up.
Marvin Grow up.
Officer What you need is a steady relationship.
Marvin How do I get one of those?
Officer Have a look around. See what takes your fancy.
Marvin First glance like?
Officer Exactly.
Marvin Right.

The strobe/freezelite comes on for not more than ten seconds as the Company change for the next scene. Link theme tune "First Time"

Song: First Glance

The strobe/freezelite stops and the Lights come up to reveal Singer standing DR. *There is a small Backing Group. A spot picks out a lamppost with a bench* L

There is a mimed dumb show during the song; movements are given below each single line of lyric, or lines of lyric. The movements should be bold but without undue exaggeration

Single tone. The freeze is broken. Action and sound start

Singer Looks like a girl who's got
All of the world in her sights.

Marvin enters L, *walks to the lamppost and stands in the pool of light. He is nervous, looks at his watch, freezes on the word "sights"*

>   Walks like a queen and is
>   Every boy's dream in the night.

Marvin's girl enters R *and walks* C. *She does her face. She freezes on "night"*

>   Treat me like dirt and you make my heart hurt
>   With your talk,
>   Run me around but I worship the ground
>   That you walk.
>   But please don't laugh.

The freeze is broken

>   First glance I thought that
>   The girl I had caught was indeed,
>   An angel of light that had dazzled the sight within me.
>   But then I saw that the girl I adored was not true,
>   Her wings were not white but as dark as the night
>   And I knew.
>   But please don't laugh.

As the freeze breaks they meet C. *She offers her cheek, he pecks. She scolds him for lateness. He takes a small gift from his pocket. Her mood changes. She likes it. She opens the box, takes out and hold up a gold chain necklace*

   A Girl Friend of Marvin's Girl enters. She is a bit thick, chews gum, flashy dresser

Marvin's Girl shows her Girl Friend the necklace. Reaction from Girl Friend: "It's really nice!" All freeze on the word "but"

>   First glance is all that I based my heart on.
>   Thought that would be quite enough.
>   But then I found that there's more than first looks.
>   Your life, I could take
>   So you can't cause heartaches again.

On the word "glance", Marvin's Girl shows that she has no cigarettes. Marvin shows that he is willing to go and get some for her. She offers money—no, he'll pay for them

   Marvin exits on "heartaches again"

The two girls freeze

>   First glance is all that I based my heart on.
>   Thought that would be quite enough.
>   But then I found that there's more than first looks.
>   Your life, I could take
>   So you can't cause heartaches again.

On the word "glance" the freeze is broken as two other boys enter. They chat up the girls. They all exit on "but then I found"

First Time

Marvin enters on "first looks", stops dead in his tracks as he sees them leave. Dejected, he stays in a freeze until the end of the song. The Lights fade on Marvin

The strobe/freezelite comes on for not more than ten seconds as the Company change for the next scene. Link theme tune "First Time"

Sketch: First Kiss

The strobe/freezelite stops and the Lights come up to reveal Marvin and Tom (his old schoolmate from "First Fag"). They are standing in the park. The lamppost has gone, the bench has been moved to R. *There is a sign "Keep Off The Grass" and a larger sign* L *"Public Park". There is a waste-bin by the bench*

Single tone. The freeze is broken. Action and sound start

Marvin Thanks for comin' Tom.
Tom That's all right. (*A slight pause*) What are mates for?
Marvin I mean it.
Tom Yeah, I know you do. (*A slight pause; he looks at his watch*) Let's have a look at that photo again.

Marvin gets out a photograph

Nice.
Marvin You think so?
Tom I wouldn't mind a crack at it.
Marvin Her mate gave it to me. It's only a passport photograph but she looks all right doesn't she?
Tom Very nice. Julie?
Marvin Yeah.
Tom (*returning the photo*) She's gorgeous. (*He looks at his watch*) She's late.
Marvin Doesn't matter.
Tom Tell her off when she comes.

Marvin laughs

I mean it. Start out how you mean to go on.
Marvin I can't tell her off on our first date. (*Pause*) What shall I talk about?
Tom Anything—but make sure you get her phone number and address.
Marvin Won't be easy.
Tom Course it will.
Marvin I'm not very good at chatting birds up.
Tom Don't worry. You probably won't get a word in edgeways once she starts rabbiting.
Marvin Won't I?
Tom No. Once they start, they can't stop.
Marvin I hope you're right.
Tom Course I am. Look, here she comes. (*He nods off in her direction*)
Marvin You sure. Where? (*He screws up his eyes*)
Tom Along the path.
Marvin I can't see her.

Tom Well, put your glasses on.

Marvin takes out his glasses and puts them on

Marvin Oh God—it is her.
Tom I said it was.

Marvin puts his glasses away

Why don't you keep your glasses on?
Marvin I look stupid.
Tom You're blind without them.
Marvin Don't go until I've introduced you.
Tom She could get up and walk away and you'd never know!
Marvin Shut up.
Tom Look. Take her for a drink or a meal or something. I shall be coming back through the park in a while and I don't want to find you sitting here talkin' to yourself.
Marvin I'm not wearing my glasses!
Tom Suit yourself.

Julie enters

Marvin Hi.
Julie Hello. Sorry I'm late.

Marvin stares at her. Tom gently nudges Marvin

Marvin (*jolted out of his dream*) Oh yeah. Er . . . Julie this is my mate Tom . . . who I just happened to bump into a couple of minutes ago.
Julie Hello.
Tom Please to meet you. (*Pause*) Well . . . I'd better be off.
Marvin See you around Tom.
Tom Right. Bye.
Julie Goodbye.

Tom exits

Pause

Marvin Would you like to sit down—for a bit. (*He realizes the misinterpretation*) I mean—for a while. It's a nice evening.
Julie Yes. I don't mind.

They sit

It's a nice park.
Marvin (*squinting out front*) Yes. I often come here. It's close to my home. (*Pause*) You don't have to come if you don't want to.
Julie What?
Marvin Come out tonight. I'm glad you did, but——
Julie (*interrupting*) No. I wanted to come. I'm pleased you asked me.

Pause. Julie smiles at Marvin. Their attention is distracted by . . .

First Time

The entrance of Old Gertie who is carrying some paper-wrapped chips. Gertie sits next to Marvin and Julie and eats them

A long pause

Julie (*trying to distract from the chip-eating*) Lovely flowers.
Marvin Yes.

Pause

Gertie They're tulips.
Julie Yes.

A slight pause

Gertie From Holland.
Julie They're lovely.
Gertie (*nodding to her left*) Over there they have fields upon fields of them.

Marvin tries hard to see in the direction she has nodded

Julie Where?
Gertie Holland.

A long pause

Marvin What would you like to do tonight?
Julie I don't mind.
Marvin I don't mind either. I thought maybe——
Gertie (*interrupting*) Take her for a meal ...

Marvin stares at Gertie eating her chips

Marvin Would you like to go for a meal?
Julie I don't mind if that's what you want to do.
Marvin I don't mind either.
Gertie (*screwing up her paper and bunging it in the bin*) Heaven preserve us!

Gertie exits

Marvin and Julie smile at each other

Julie I got a letter from Iris today.
Marvin Iris?
Julie You know, my friend that arranged this date.
Marvin Oh, Iris!
Julie She's in Devon.
Marvin Nice.
Julie On holiday. (*After a pause*) Would you like to read her letter?
Marvin Sure.

Julie takes out a letter and hands it to Marvin

Julie Have you known her long?
Marvin No, not really. She's a friend of Tom's, you know, my mate you met earlier.

Julie Oh yes.

Marvin tries to read it but it's useless without his glasses, so after squinting for a while, he pretends to read it

Have you got to that bit about the funny little donkey?
Marvin (*gently laughing*) Yeah.
Julie (*her face remaining passive*) That got run over?
Marvin (*his face changing, suddenly serious*) Yeah. (*He nods solemnly*)
Julie Shame wasn't it?
Marvin Terrible.

A slight pause

Julie Is there a restaurant you'd particularly like to go to? Chinese? Indian?
Marvin Er, no . . .
Julie It's just . . .
Marvin We don't have to go.
Julie It's just—I'd rather sit here and——

Tina enters. She is a tarty friend of Julie's

Tina (*effusively*) Julie!
Julie Oh, hello.
Tina Surprise, surprise.
Julie Yes.
Tina What are you doing out here?
Julie Oh Tina. This is Marvin. Marvin—Tina.
Tina Hello Marvin.

Marvin stands to shake hands but Tina whips past him and sits in his place next to Julie

Marvin Hi.
Tina I'm not interrupting anything am I?
Julie No. We were just chatting.
Marvin Lovely evening.
Tina (*a bit bored with Marvin*) Yeah, It's been really hot today ain't it?
Julie Yes.
Marvin Boiling.
Tina (*not impressed*) Yeah. (*Back to Julie excitedly*) You'll never guess who I saw today?
Julie Who?
Tina Pat.

Julie can't recall her

Remember, Pat from school. First one in the year to get a bra.
Julie Oh—that Pat.
Tina Yeah. She's engaged now. Guess who to?
Julie (*thinking*) Mmmmmmm.
Tina You'll never guess.
Julie (*still thinking*) Errr.

First Time

Tina Never in a month of Sundays.
Julie (*brightly*) David.
Tina (*sneering*) Nah ... Alan!
Julie Alan? (*She can't recall the name*)
Tina Alan—from school. The first one in the year to take Pat's bra off.
Julie Oh—that Alan.
Tina Surprise eh?
Julie Yes.
Tina I'm on my way over to her now, meeting her at the pub. Why don't you come? All the girls that were with us in the fifth year'll be there.
Julie (*signifying Marvin*) Well, I can't ...
Tina Both of you come.
Marvin That's very kind of you.
Tina Unless of course you had something else planned?
Marvin No. (*Disappointed*) No.
Tina Then come on.
Julie (*disappointed as well*) Well?
Tina You don't mind Marvin, do you?
Marvin (*gallant*) Not at all.
Tina I can see you're a good sort.
Marvin (*lying*) Actually I have got somewhere else to go.
Julie (*surprised*) Have you?
Marvin Yes. Not planned, but it was an invitation left open.
Tina (*delighted*) See.
Marvin Some friends are leaving work. I said I'd try and make it if I could.
Tina Well that's settled, Julie. *We* can have a really good old chinwag and *Marvin* can see his mates off.
Julie You don't mind?
Marvin Not if you want to go.
Tina 'Ere you two could do wiv an evening off from each other. How long you been together now? A couple of months I bet. When I come along I could see you was bored.
Julie (*last appeal*) Marvin?
Marvin No, it's fine. You go along and enjoy yourself. It'll be great to see some of my mates at the leaving party.
Tina (*standing*) Right. Come on Julie.
Julie You're sure you don't mind.
Tina (*sensing a loss*) 'Ere, why don't you join us later, eh?
Marvin (*forced smile*) Good idea. I might well get along later.

Julie stands and drops her spectacle case. She is embarrassed

Tina Gawd. Now you've dropped your glasses. (*To Marvin*) She was exactly the same at school, Marvin. "Blinkers" we used to call her.

Marvin bends down, picks up the glasses and hands them to Julie

Julie (*quietly*) Thanks.
Tina We might see you later on then.
Marvin Yes.

Tina Bye.
Marvin Bye.

Tina and Julie exit

Pause

Tom enters

Tom (*spotting the girls going*) Where's she off to? What's that wiv 'er? Marvin. (*He sits beside Marvin*) Where's she gone?
Marvin Don't know.
Tom What went wrong?

Gertie is on her way back. She mistakes Tom for Julie

Marvin Don't know that either.
Gertie (*en passant*) Take her for a meal.
Tom You what?

Gertie exits, followed by Tom

Song: A Woman

Marvin
Was it meant to be this way,
Always on my own.
People suffer more than me,
Perhaps I shouldn't moan.
But if I could change my life,
I know what I would want.
You to spend a night with me.
I like you, do you like me?
I've never loved a woman and I guess I never,
Looks like I never will.

Friends have said they'd like to be
Single once again.
But if they knew what I felt
They'd not swop with me.
Julie I tried to make you mine.
Only for a while.
You were my dream girl I thought I had found.
A girl that would make me feel happy and proud.
I've never loved a woman and I guess I never,
Looks like I never, will.

Julie enters wearing glasses. She stops and listens to Marvin sing

You to spend a night with me.
I like you, do you like me?
I've never loved a woman and I guess I never,
Looks like I never, will.

Marvin steps away from the microphone. He can't see her. He puts on his

First Time 35

glasses. She moves towards him. Tight spot. She leans forward and kisses him on the cheek. He stands still. They look at each other

She drops the hand at the side of his face, turns and walks off slowly

As he watches her go the Lights fade slowly. Black-out, Marvin exits. There is a moment ... then the Lights come up as Marvin and Tom enter, talking as they cross the stage

Tom In what way, Marvin?
Marvin Sorry?
Tom In what way do you feel funny?
Marvin Well ... tired. All the time. Run down, that sort of funny.
Tom Have you been to the doctors?
Marvin Why. Do you think I should?
Tom Maybe ... maybe it's love.
Marvin Love?
Tom Yeah. You still seeing Julie?
Marvin We're engaged.
Tom (*incredulous*) What! To get married?
Marvin Well we're not engaged to get divorced!
Tom Change the subject. I see Torquay lost at the weekend.
Marvin Torquay lose every weekend.
Tom What a team to support.
Marvin I've had funny dreams as well.
Tom As well as what?
Marvin As well as feeling funny.
Tom Funny dreams?
Marvin Yes. You know I'm going on this cycling holiday.
Tom With Julie?
Marvin Yes. With Julie. Why do you keep bringing her into it?
Tom Go on.
Marvin Well, the other night I dreamt we'd gone on this holiday. It was like some daft nightmare. It started with this old bloke saying how Julie and I had found "true love".

The strobe/freezelite comes on for not more than ten seconds as the Company change for the next scene. Link theme tune "First Time"

Sketch: First Bite

The strobe/freezelite stops, and the Lights come up to reveal the interior of a gothic castle. There is a piano R *and a huge throne-like chair draped in gauze, but any other scenery added would be purely for atmosphere. The sense of spookiness should be created merely by lighting and standard B-movie horror film costumes. A plethora of cloaks, deformed backs and white gauze gowns Single tone. The freeze is broken. Action and sound start*

A spotlight picks up the Narrator standing L. *He has a large storybook in his hand*

Narrator And so Marvin and Julie had at last found true love—that emotional bond which was to unite them closely for at least—six months. And what a six months! A period of whirlwind romance that was to culminate in a round-Europe cycling holiday. But little did they realize the danger that awaited them ...

A green light comes up on the Narrator

... as they cycled into the tiny tranquil village of **Bogoff** nestling snugly beneath the towering mountains of inner Transylvania, gently counting the years. Shoulder to shoulder with Old Father Time, it seemed much the same as any other tiny tranquil village nestling snugly beneath the towering mountains of inner Transylvania. But then why shouldn't it? True, it had once been the scene of satanic rites and barbaric atrocities beyond equal in the civilized world. True, bodies had been found pierced by two unaccountably strange teeth marks below the left ear and true the superstitious local peasants still refused to venture out after dark, terrified by the absurd rumours that the undead still walked the forest paths searching for a midnight snack ... but this was a—long—time—ago. (*He turns and starts to walk on to the raised area*) After all, the old crumbling castle on—(*suddenly he stops, turns and speaks in sinister tones*)—Blood Drip Crag had long been deserted. Or had it?

The Narrator exits

A crack of thunder followed by lightning

Marvin and Julie enter. Marvin is carrying a bicycle wheel with a punctured tyre. They are dressed in shorts and holiday tops

Julie Marvin. Marvin. Wait for me.
Marvin Here you are Julie. Just as I said. A castle.
Julie I'm not so sure, Marvin.
Marvin Of course it's a castle.
Julie I mean I'm not so sure we should have come here.
Marvin Trust me Julie. We will ask the people within whether or not they have a spare inner tube for a Raleigh six-speed and if not perhaps they will put us up for the night and tomorrow we will continue our (*in one breath*) round-Europe-careful-to-avoid-the-autobahns-cycling-trip.
Julie (*speaking out front*) Very well, Marvin. You seem to know what you're doing.
Marvin Trust me.
Julie Shouldn't we ring?
Marvin They may not have a phone.
Julie I mean the bell. (*She nods toward the imaginary door*)
Marvin (*side-spies out front*) Good idea.

Marvin rings the "doorbell" and we hear the sound of a British Telecom telephone. They smile at each other nervously

Jackie Boy enters—a hunched-back butler. He is covered in dust, cobwebs and filthy bits and pieces. He opens the door a small crack and there is a small creaking sound

First Time

Butler Hi! I'm Jackie Boy the butler. (*He has a fixed inane grin on his face the whole time regardless of his dialogue or stage action*)
Marvin Hi.
Butler You must be——
Marvin Lost?
Butler —wet. Standing out there. Please come in.

There is a deafeningly loud sound of a huge door creaking open. It takes a long time to open but shuts quickly without a sound. The butler mimes the door process

Marvin Thanks.
Julie Cheers.
Butler Thirsty?
Marvin Well.
Julie Marvin?
Marvin Trust me.
Butler No doubt you wish——
Julie I'm scared.
Butler —to stay the night.
Marvin Yes.

The Butler's grin disappears immediately

Er, that is please ...

Pause

Thank you very much ...

Pause

A lot ...

The grin returns

Butler Good. (*He calls off*) Esmerelda!

A clatter of bells being dropped. A deformed servant girl enters. She has long black hair and is filthy dirty

Go and get the master and stop playing with those bells. (*He kicks her*)

Esmerelda exits with a hideous howl

This way, sir.
Julie Marvin.
Marvin Trust me. (*Going to the Butler*) Look, all we really——
Butler Have you travelled far?
Marvin From England. We're on a cycling holiday.
Butler How ... quaint.
Marvin Actually we've had a puncture.
Butler That's what they all say.

Mother enters. She is a lunatic

Mother What do they want?
Butler This is the master's mother.
Mother I know who I am. Who are they?
Marvin This is Julie and I am Marvin.
Julie Hi.
Marvin We're on a cycling holiday. Taking in all the historical sights that one would usually miss travelling by car.
Mother So?
Marvin (*after a pause*) So ... we've had a puncture and were wondering——
Mother (*at tremendous lunatic speed*) If this castle had any strange stories to reveal; headless huntsmen, vanishing ladies, breastless maids, castrated footmen? I know what you want. You want to unearth gory details from the past. To disturb murky secrets buried in the vaults of time. You're like all the others. Not content with a quick cup of tea, a biscuit and then on your bike. No. You have to stay the night in some dusty old bedroom that hasn't been used since the old mistress cut off her foot, shaving her leg.

2 Asylum Assistants in white coats enter

Then in the morning one of you has vanished and the other insists on calling in some lunatic expert who has a theory about the *undead* and who proceeds to stick little bits of wood into the chest of any unfortunate creep who has crept into the crypt for a kip!

The attendants pick her up and carry her off, shouting back

Bloody travelling salesmen!
Butler (*grinning*) Sorry about that.

Esmerelda enters

What is it?

Esmerelda whispers in the Butler's ear. The noise is grotesque like someone eating gooey porridge

Very well. Stay here. And don't go wandering off.

He kicks Esmerelda who makes disgusting noises

And they'd (*pointing at Marvin and Julie*) better be in one piece when I get back. (*To Marvin and Julie*) Excuse me.

The Butler exits

Julie Marvin.
Marvin I know.

They look at Esmerelda—noises

Trust me.

Count Alucard enters. He has been cooking. He wears an apron with the logo "Feed the World" on it. His hands are covered in flour. He has a rolling pin, which he hands to the deformed servant. He is slightly camp

Alucard (*as he sweeps in*) Oh. I'm so terribly sorry.
Marvin Sorry?
Alucard About the puncture.
Marvin Oh.
Alucard Jackie just told me. You must have been terribly distressed.
Marvin Er, yes.
Alucard What a shame. On your "hols" too.

Esmerelda is pulling the hem of Marvin's shorts intermittently

Julie Yes.
Alucard Poor dears. I bet you were furious.
Marvin Well it was rather annoying wasn't it, Julie?

Alucard spots Esmerelda pulling at the trousers

Alucard Esmerelda! What do you want?

Esmerelda whispers in Alucard's ear

Don't be so revolting! Go straight to your room.

Esmerelda exits

And no tea! I'm so sorry about that. Let me introduce myself. I am Alucard Eripmaff, Count of Depravia. I'd shake hands but I'm covered in flour. I do love to do it the Beeton way. What about you?
Marvin Well ...
Alucard Good. I'm so glad you agree. If there's anything I can do for you, please don't hesitate to ask. (*He starts to go*)
Marvin Well, that's very kind of you. I wonder ... could you put us up for the night?
Alucard Oh good Lord. If only I could.
Marvin You mean ...
Alucard Every room in the castle's taken.
Marvin Every room in the castle's taken?
Alucard (*looking off*) What a nasty echo.
Marvin But I thought ...
Alucard What, Marvin? What did you think? Mmm? Mmm?
Marvin Nothing. I ...
Alucard Right. Good. Any more questions? (*A slight pause*) No? Then you'd better be off.
Marvin Off?
Alucard Yes off. O—F—F. Off?
Marvin But ...
Alucard No buts. I've some baking to do and you're becoming tiresome. (*He opens the creaking door*)
Marvin But what about Julie?
Alucard She's quite safe with me.
Marvin But I can't go.
Alucard On your bike!

The sound of a huge door slamming. Marvin wanders disconsolately away

The Butler enters

Alucard Ah, Jackie Boy.
Butler (*still grinning inanely*) Master?
Alucard Take this lovely young lady to her rooms and let her slip into something much more comfortable.
Butler Certainly.

The Butler takes Julie off

Marvin runs back to the imaginary front door

The Butler enters alone

Alucard Where are the girls?
Butler Playing.

Marvin knocks on the front door. Alucard opens it with a short sharp creak

Alucard What do *you* want?
Marvin (*livid*) Someone's stolen our bikes.
Alucard Raleigh? (*Meaning "really"*)
Marvin It's not funny.
Alucard It all depends on where you're standing, dear.
Marvin We can't cycle without them.
Alucard I suppose you'd better come in.
Marvin They're Raleigh six-speed drophandlebar lightweights with aluminium frames.
Alucard }
Butler   } (*together*) "I was so impressed I bought the company."
Alucard Shut up Marvin. You're becoming a bore.

Two giggling Maids ride across upstage behind the action on bicycles. New toys

Marvin What am I going to do?
Alucard (*together, walking towards him in unison, two steps, closely side by*
Butler   *side like Siamese twins*) I suppose you'll have to stay.
Marvin But what about our bikes?
Alucard }
Butler   } (*together, one step forward as before*) They can stay too.
Marvin Oh damn.
Alucard Language.
Butler Shall I show him the spare room?
Alucard Oh, go on. If you must.

The Butler produces a photograph of the spare room

Do you like it? I chose the wallpaper.
Marvin (*suddenly realizing Julie is not there*) Julie!
Alucard John Lewis mix 'n match. Cost a fortune.
Marvin Where's my Julie?
Alucard Oh, it's *your* Julie now is it? Five minutes ago you ran off and left her.

First Time

Marvin Never!
Alucard Oh, you fibber.
Marvin You threw me out.
Alucard (*aghast*) I never touched you.
Butler Shall I kick him in the naughty parts, master?
Alucard No! (*A slight pause*) I will! (*He kicks Marvin in the naughty parts*)
Butler Oh, good shot sir.
Alucard Thank you. I've been practising.

Julie enters with Esmerelda

Julie (*spotting Marvin*) Marvin! (*Turning on them*) What have you done to him?
Butler He attacked the master with his willy.
Alucard Straightforward self-defence I'm afraid.
Julie We wish to leave this instant.
Alucard Oh do you, Miss Bossy Boots.
Marvin (*rising*) I feel faint.
Butler Shall I kick him again, master?
Alucard No! (*A slight pause*) Oh, go on then, if you must.
Julie You just dare.

Mother enters

Mother Who's there?
Alucard God preserve us. Go to bed, Mother.
Mother Where's my dinner?
Alucard It's being stuffed.
Mother Manners, Alucard.
Alucard Sorry Mother.
Marvin Dinner?
Alucard Yes. Didn't we tell you? You're on the menu.
Mother Get on with it.
Butler Master, it's time.
Alucard Oh no! (*Sulkily*) You know I prefer the sage and onion.
Butler No master. It's time for your drink.
Alucard Oh Lord, is it? No wonder I'm feeling grumpy, grumpy grumpee!

Two Maids cycle past in the opposite direction. Giggles and noise

Marvin (*open-mouthed*) Our bikes!
Alucard It's too late for that now I'm afraid. Jackie Boy!

They sing the next lines to the tune "Derry Derry Down" and at the same time perform a funny sequence whereby Marvin finishes up over the Butler's shoulder

Butler Master?
Alucard Fare thee well?
Butler Very well.
Alucard Hey down.
Butler Ho down.

Alucard
Butler } Derry Derry Down. Among the leaves so ... (*Speaking*) Got him!

Alucard Off to the kitchen and get him ready for din-dins.

The Butler carries him off

Marvin (*calling to her*) Julie!
Julie (*calling back to him*) Marvin!
Marvin Julie.
Julie Marvin.
Marvin Julie ...
Julie Marvinnnnn ...

Marvin's cries get fainter as he is lugged off to the kitchen

Alucard He's gone.

Julie steps back from him, afraid

Penny for your thoughts, Julie. (*He throws back his cloak*)
Julie You monster!
Alucard Now you're just guessing!
Julie What are you going to do to me?
Alucard I thought we might have a little ... drink.
Julie What kind of drink?
Alucard I thought maybe a little red ...
Julie Wine?
Alucard Why not, if it makes you happy. (*He emits a loud wolfish whine—a lycanthropic howl*)
Julie Please don't take advantage of me.

Alucard moves to the piano like Liberace

The household gather on, round and under the piano

Alucard plays the piano. (There are in fact only two chords to learn) During the number Julie makes the melodramatic gestures one associates with a Victorian heroine about to be deflowered. Each gesture comes at the end of each line)

Song: Jugular Blues

Alucard   It's a cold moonlit night tonight,
Ideal for a flight with you, girl.
Star speckled sky, oh watch us fly,
O'er the world.
Now be a pet and bare your neck for me, girl.
I've got those jugular blues tonight.
Only a pint of your blood will put me right
Don't get left on the shelf
Don't keep your blood to yourself
No need to holler, just open up your collar.
One bite and I'll swaller your love.
Don't keep your blood to yourself.

First Time

The following duologue is spoken over the music reprise

(*Speaking*) Anything wrong?
Julie You frighten me.
Alucard Nonsense.
Julie I thought you might be——
Alucard What?
Julie —a vampire——

Alucard is shocked into playing a fumbled number of discordant chords. He slams down the lid of the piano

—one of those creatures——
Alucard (*standing quickly*) Yes?
Julie —that live off the *blood*——

Alucard jumps up on the piano stool with a squeak

—of *helpless*——

He jumps on top of the piano

—*mortals*——

He flaps his cloak like wings and jumps off the piano in a vain attempt to fly

Alucard (*landing suddenly; cool*) Perish the thought.
Julie —that suck blood from the neck—just here.
Alucard (*looking at her neck longingly*) I know the sort!
Julie But! They hate *garlic*! (*She breathes on him*)
Alucard Agghhh!
Julie Fear the sign of the cross—— (*She makes the sign of the cross with her fingers*)
Alucard More agghhh!
Julie —and are terrified by the rays of the sun!

She opens imaginary window curtains also making the sound of curtains opening. The Lights suddenly brighten. Alucard closes them equally quickly, making a similar sound

Alucard Silly girl! Whatever gave you that impression?
Julie But they can be destroyed with the wooden *stake*.
Alucard Don't let's get morbid. Look into my eyes.
Julie I can't.
Alucard You must.
Julie Why?
Alucard Because this nightmare will grind to a halt if you don't.
Julie Very well.
Alucard (*singing*) You look lovely tonight,
                   A real delight.
                   Feel thirsty or fancy a bite.
                   You make me feel so goo-ood!
                   What a lovely complexion you've got,
                   Sort of rosy red,

>   Let's not beat about the bush
>   Fancy a pint?
>   You make me feel so goo-ood!
>
>   I've got those jugular blues tonight
>   Only a pint of your blood will put me right
>   Don't get left on the shelf
>   Don't keep your blood to yourself.
>   No need to holler, just open up your collar
>   One bite and I'll swaller your love
>   Don't keep your blood to yourself.

The Chorus hum a reprise of the chorus under the ensuing action

>   Look into my eyes and I will give you life after death.

Julie Don't be preposterous.

Marvin enters. He has been badly beaten up, a wreck of a man, very funny. He holds a wooden stake and a mallet in his raised hand

Alucard (*spotting him*) No. No.
Marvin Yes, yes. Take that!

Marvin knocks the stake in, which Alucard holds in position. There is a hollow sound as the stake is hit

>   DRACULAAA!

Alucard How did you guess my identity?
Marvin Easy. (*Out front*) Alucard Eripmaff spells Dracula Ffampire backwards.
Alucard You killjoy!

There ensues the longest and most complicated death of all time, involving much horror and enranged stumbling around the stage area. The rest of the cast realize what is about to happen and take out books to read, fall asleep, play cards, start writing letters, make tea and totally ignore Alucard until he says:

>   Ready?

All (*bored*) Yeah. (*They sing*)
>   I've got those jugular blues tonight
>   Only a pint of your blood will put me right
>   Don't get left on the shelf
>   Don't keep your blood to yourself.
>   No need to holler, just open up your collar

Alucard One bite and I'll swaller your love
>   Don't keep your blood to yourself. (*He dies*)

Marvin So ends his dreadful reign.

There is a terrific clap of thunder and the rain pours down. The Company produce umbrellas, raise them and exit at high speed to the theme music and strobe

The strobe and the House Lights come up

SECOND HALF

Song: First Time (Reprise)

Reprise of first verse and chorus of "First Time" sung by Marvin and Julie. As they sing this number the Company take their places at their chairs and get ready for the first number. At the end of the reprise ...

The strobe/freezelite comes on for not more than ten seconds as the Company change for the next scene. Link theme tune "First Time"

Song: First Time I Saw You

The strobe/freezelite stops and the Lights come up to reveal a street. R *we see Sid (from "First Fag") sitting at an imaginary dressing table. He is doing his hair for a night out on the town. The actions are mime-like—a living tableau*

Single tone. The freeze is broken. Action and sound start

Company Ooo-Ooo-Ooo-Ooo
Ooo-Ooo-Ooo-Ooo
What's your problem girl?
Ooo-Ooo-Ooo-Ooo
Ooo-Ooo-Ooo-Ooo
What's your problem girl?

During this intro Sid finishes his hair, puts on his coat, and ventures out

Two Girls enter and walk to the street corner. One of the girls has a large bag that hides a huge pair of feet. The other girl walks to conceal the fact that she has a huge hunched back, by walking sideways but in a natural fashion thus concealing the lump from the audience. They finish up at C

First time I saw you, you were out with a friend,

Sid comes over and spots the girls

Dressed up to kill and looking for men.
I went over to you at the end of the street.

Sid chats up the two girls

That's when I noticed the size of your feet.

Girl 1 lifts up her bag. She is standing side on, wearing huge boots

Her friend then looked better and I gave her the wink.

Sid winks at her

I edged over to her. But boy did she stink.

Sid shows she suffers from BO
>I said that her friend I would soon dump.

Sid means the girl with the feet
>It was then that I noticed

Girl 2 turns sideways to console Girl 1 and reveals her hump
>The size of her hump.
>Out of the frying pan into the fire.

Sid moves DC
>I had to quench my sensual desire.
>I'd rather the feet than the hump on the back,

Sid returns to the girl with the feet
>It was then that I noticed her teeth were all black.

Girl 1 smiles to reveal black teeth
>Then on came old Norman

Nutty Norman (from "First Fag") enters, wearing a flasher mac and cap
>And I told him the laugh,
>He looked at the girls and said I was daft.

Norman speaks "You're daft, mate."
>The one with the big hump and the one with the feet
>He pulled back his mac

Norman flashes—his back to the audience
>And they followed like sheep.

Norman and the Girls exit

Company ⎱ I was so silly and fussy to boot.
Sid ⎰ They didn't look bad and were really quite cute.
>Now I'm alone and a lonely old man.

A "camp" guy walks past
>The moral of this story is Take What You Can

Sid starts to follow him off. Returning in the opposite direction is Norman with the Girls. Norman gives a quick flash to the camp guy and he joins their party immediately

Sid is left alone
>Ooo-Ooo-Ooo-Ooo
>What's your problem girl?

Marvin and Julie enter—they show Sid the engagement ring—will he be their best man? He agrees. They pin a buttonhole on his jacket and freeze

First Time

>Ooo-Ooo-Ooo-Ooo
>What's your problem girl?

The Company freeze as the strobe/freezelite comes on for not more than ten seconds as the Company change for the first scene. Link theme tune "First Time"

Sketch: First Wife

The strobe/freezelite stops and the Lights come up to reveal the Best Man and Marvin's Father, an older Paul. The Vicar enters. They are outside the church where Marvin and Julie are about to be married. Off-stage we hear a cheerful hymn being played as a voluntary

Single tone. The freeze is broken. Action and sound start

Vicar All ready?
Marvin's Dad No.
Vicar Good. (*A double-take*) What?
Best Man There's no bride.
Marvin's Dad And no bridegroom.
Vicar Why not?
Best Man I don't know.
Vicar I was about to start.
Marvin's Dad You'll look a right wally if you do.
Vicar Oh dear.
Marvin's Dad Get them to play another tune—while we wait.
Best Man (*having spotted the bride*) "Here comes the bride".
Vicar We can't play that yet.
Best Man Oh God. Where is he?
Marvin's Dad She'll have to drive round the church again.

Julie enters with her Father and two Bridesmaids who fidget all the time

Best Man He's not here.
Julie's Dad What do you mean? He's not here.
Julie Dad.
Julie's Dad Our Julie's here.
Marvin's Dad Well our Marvin isn't.
Julie's Dad Why not? That's what I want to know.
Vicar That's what we all want to know.
Julie's Dad Who the hell are you?
Vicar I'm the vicar.
Julie's Dad (*aggressively*) So?
Vicar (*sensing danger*) I think I'd better go in.

The Vicar enters the church. We hear a classical tune played

Julie Dad.
Julie's Dad All right Julie. We're going to go for a short drive.
Best Man I think that's for the best.
Julie's Dad I think he'd better be here when we get back.

Bride's party exit, the Bridesmaids squabbling, all sense of occasion lost

The Photographer enters

Photographer Ready for the photos?
Marvin's Dad I am—but we seem to have lost the happy couple.
Photographer The what?
Best Man The bride and groom.
Photographer Oh dearie me. What a kerfuffle.

The Bride's Mum leaves the church. She is distraught and accompanied by a kindly Sister

Julie's Mum Where's my daughter?
Marvin's Dad I've no idea.
Best Man I have.
Julie's Mum Where is she?
Marvin's Dad Just driven off.
Best Man For a short drive.
Julie's Mum Where's Marvin?
Photographer Good question. I'll just check my camera.
Julie's Mum He won't be in there.

The Photographer exits

Will you give me a proper answer!
Marvin's Dad / **Best Man** (*shouting together*) We don't know!

Julie's Mum is dumbfounded

The Vicar reappears

Vicar Come in. Everything will be all right.

Marvin's Dad bursts into laughter

Marvin's Dad Sorry. I thought it was a joke.

They all enter the church apart from Marvin's Dad and the Best Man

Marvin's Dad produces a hip-flask and takes a swig

Best Man I didn't want to be Marvin's best man in the first place.
Marvin's Dad I didn't want Marvin in the first place.

The tune of the funeral march is heard coming from the church interior

Best Man He's a pain.
Marvin's Dad Aren't you supposed to be with him?
Best Man How can I be with him. I haven't laid eyes on him for two days.
Marvin's Dad Oh dear.

The Vicar enters

Vicar Any luck?
Marvin's Dad No. We're still here.
Best Man Should be here soon.

First Time

Marvin's Dad Play another tune.
Vicar I do hope they hurry.
Marvin's Dad Sounds appropriate. Beatles' number is it?
Best Man Here they come again.

The church organ plays "She Loves You"

The Bride's party enters again. The Bridesmaids have ice-lollies

Julie's Dad Well?
Marvin's Dad Not very.
Julie's Dad Is he here?
Best Man Not really.
Julie Dad.
Julie's Dad Listen. If he's not here in five minutes, the wedding's off.
Julie Dad.
Julie's Dad Come on.

They start to leave and meet the Photographer coming back

Photographer Ready?
Julie's Dad Clear off!

The Bride's party exit to the church

Photographer I say.

Marvin's Dad leans into the Photographer clutching his flask

Marvin's Dad Tipple?
Photographer Higgins actually, High Street. Photos. Here's my card.

He hands him a card. Marvin's Dad hands him his flask

Marvin's Dad Here's my bottle.
Photographer Don't mind if I do.
Best Man I wish you'd start helping.
Marvin's Dad What do you want me to do?
Best Man Panic and keep me company.

Julie's Mum enters with the kindly consoling Sister

The organ plays something like "Rock Around the Clock"

Julie's Mum Are they here?
Marvin's Dad Been ... and gone.

Julie's Mum bursts into tears and exits with the Sister

Best Man You could have been a bit more diplomatic.
Marvin's Dad I'm a mechanic, not a bleedin' politician.
Photographer Oh, very droll.
Marvin's Dad (*snatching back his flask*) And I'm not your doll.

In unison they look off

Photographer I say. Is that him?

Best Man Where?
Photographer By that gravestone.
Best Man Oh God.
Photographer Is it?
Marvin's Dad (*calling*) Hello ... Marvin.
Best Man Oh God.
Photographer I must get my camera.

The Photographer exits

Best Man Where have you been?

Marvin enters slightly the worse for drink, his wedding clothes dishevelled

Best Man Marvin?
Marvin Sid?
Best Man Hell.
Marvin (*perplexed as if it's a quiz*) Heaven!
Best Man What are you talking about?
Marvin I thought it was one of those word association tests. Hello Dad.
Marvin's Dad Hello son.
Marvin Hello Dad.
Marvin's Dad Fancy a drink?
Marvin No, it's all right. (*Slurred speech*) I've had one.
Best Man We've got to get him in.
Marvin's Dad Of course.
Marvin I'm sorry I'm late.
Marvin's Dad I'm not. It's been great out here.

The Bride's Mum, Sister, Friends and Vicar enter

Julie's Mum Is he here? ... Aagh! (*She shrieks*)
Vicar (*seeing father and son drunk*) Good God!
Marvin's Dad I'm sure he is, vicar.
Julie's Mum He's ... he's ...
Marvin's Dad Marvin. Yes ... very good.
Best Man It'll be all right if we just get him into church.

The Vicar shouts into the church

Vicar Play another tune.
Julie's Mum He looks drunk to me.

The organ plays the latest hit tune

Marvin That's 'cos I am.
Best Man Vicar. We must get everyone inside.
Vicar Right.
Julie's Mum My husband.
Marvin My wife.
Vicar My God!

Julie enters. The Bridesmaids are fighting and arguing, their clothes

First Time

wrecked. They are accompanied by Julie's Dad, the Photographer and other wedding guests

Julie's Dad Is he here?... Aaaah!
Julie Dad... Marvin.
Marvin Mum, er... thingy. (*He can't remember Julie's name*)
Julie Dad.
Julie's Mum I'm going to faint.
Marvin's Dad I think I'll go in.
Photographer Smile.
All Naff off!
Photographer Charming.

We hear a discordant chord on the organ, then the lid slamps. A very short, bossy Organist enters. Silence

Organist Look. If I have to play another flippin' tune, I'll go barmy. If we'd known it was going to be like this we could all have stayed at 'ome and listened to tapes. Now, what is it going to be? A wedding or a bleedin' disco?

They all look down, embarrassed, then mumble

All Wedding!
Organist (*shouting*) What?
All (*shouting at him*) A wedding!!
Organist (*softly*) Right.

The Organist marches back in followed by the guests and last of all Julie and her Dad. We hear "Here Comes the Bride". Five-second silence. Then we hear a huge sniff then "Aaaah" and everyone exits. As they exit they freeze every two seconds as in a wedding photograph. After five photos they go into the song

Song: We Are Just Beginning

Chorus
(*sung happily*)

We are just beginning
Don't expect too much at the start.
It's about us living,
Though they'll see us, often apart.
I can let you go away,
Knowing that you will not stay
Far away, for long.
This will make us stronger—than pain,
Closer than blood.

Julie }
Marvin }

Now we're married, things won't change,
Though to start it'll seem so strange.

Julie (*annoyed*)
Marvin

Down the pub
Home at night,
Sorry I'm late

Julie (*angry*)

I don't want to fight

Julie ⎫	We're prepared for anything
Marvin ⎭	And it's only just begun

Chorus
(all tightlipped and angry)

We are just beginning
Don't expect too much at the start.
It's about us living,
Though they'll see us, often apart.
I can let you go away,
Knowing that you will not stay
Far away, for long.
This will make us stronger—than pain
Closer than blood.

Julie	Dinner's burnt
Marvin	I tried to phone
Julie	I never see you
Marvin	Please don't moan
	Said I'm sorry
Julie	Just don't lie,
Marvin	Please don't nag
Julie	You don't even try.
Both *(angry at each other)*	Not prepared for anything And it's only just begun.

Chorus *(angry at first)*
(Softer)

(Happier)

All
(holding hands)

We are just beginning
Don't expect too much at the start.
It's about us living,
Though they'll see us, often apart.
I can let you go away,
Knowing that you will not stay
Far away, for long.
This will make us stronger—than pain,
Closer than blood.

The strobe/freezelite comes on for not more than ten seconds as the Company change for the next scene. Link theme tune "First Time"

Sketch: First Family Christmas

The strobe/freezelite stops and the Lights come up to reveal Marvin and Julie in their late forties. It's Christmas Day, early evening. We hear a quiet carol in the background that fades as the scene starts. Their youngest daughter Sonia is at the table doing a jigsaw. Grandad (Paul) and Grandma (Sally) are sitting by the fire. Julie is knitting, Marvin smoking his pipe. All are wearing Christmas cracker hats. They are exhausted and glum. It is quiet. The audience will laugh because of the sudden passing of the years, so wait before ...

Single tone. The freeze is broken. Action and sound start. There is no obvious sudden movement after the freeze

First Time

Grandad (*remembering his past*) A few lumps of coal. That's all we got.
Grandma (*bored with reminiscence*) So you said.
Grandad If we were lucky. (*Pause*) But it was still fun. (*Pause*) A joyous occasion. The birth of Christ. That's what people forget nowadays. They forget what it's all about. Peace to mankind. Love and peace to your fellow humans.
Grandma Shut up, you silly old sod!
Grandad See what I mean.
Julie (*shocked*) Mum!
Grandma Well, going on and on about what it used to be like.
Julie Perhaps Grandad's right.
Grandma Course he isn't. How would he have known? He was always paralytic before Christmas dinner.
Grandad I wasn't.
Grandma Yes you were.
Grandad I was drinking to be ... sociable.
Grandma Sociable! You were so drunk you couldn't even speak.
Grandad Oh for Gawd's sake woman!
Julie (*speaking to Marvin who is in a dream*) Marvin, do you want a sandwich?
Marvin What?
Julie Sandwich.
Marvin Not for me, ta.

A slight pause

Julie (*suspicious*) Is that your jigsaw Sonia, or Sarah's?
Marvin I was just thinking, how quiet it was.
Julie Enjoy it while you can.
Marvin I wonder if they'll win?
Grandad Who?
Marvin Torquay.
Grandad Torquay never win. It's written into their contracts. "Under no circumstances will you win. Any player or players caught scoring a goal ... will be sacked on the spot!"
Marvin That would really make my Christmas.
Grandma (*genuinely concerned*) The last thing *you* want, Marvin, is excitement.
Grandad Well don't worry about that. There's very little chance of Torquay supplying any excitement.

Sudden argument off-stage

Jane (*off*) They're mine. And you know they are.
Sarah (*off*) They are not.
Jane (*off*) Mum!
Julie Here we go.
Grandma Are those girls arguing again?

Jane and Sarah storm in

Jane Mum. Sarah's got my knickers on.
Sarah No I haven't.
Jane You have.
Sarah They are not your knickers.
Jane Mum, tell her.
Grandma Girls. It's Christmas Day.
Jane (*appealing to Marvin*) Dad.
Julie Sarah, give her back her knickers.
Grandma (*suddenly turning on Grandad*) This is your fault.
Grandad My fault?
Grandma You wrapped up the same colour for both of them.
Jane Yours are on the bed.
Sarah No, they are not on the bed.
Jane Dad!
Grandma Don't upset your dad, you know he hasn't been well.

Sarah spots Sonia playing

Sarah And that's my jigsaw.
Sonia No it's not, it's mine.
Julie Sarah!
Jane Dad!
Julie Jane!
Sonia Mum!
Julie Sonia!

Stephen enters. He speaks slowly in a monotone

Stephen Right. Who sat on my Dire Straits LP?
Julie Oh God.
Jane Sarah did.
Sarah I did not.
Stephen Well someone has.
Sarah Sonia. That's my jigsaw.
Sonia (*running to Marvin*) Dad!
Stephen Please do not let us get sidetracked from the important issue. Who sat on my Dire Straits?
Jane Mum. My knickers have got butterflies on.
Sarah So have mine.
Grandma (*to Grandad*) See what you've done.
Jane These are my knickers.
Sarah Then where are mine?
Julie Marvin.
Grandad It's no good talking to him. He's got Torquay on his mind.

Sarah comes over to Sonia who is sprawled over Marvin

Julie Marvin, never mind the flaming football.
Sarah Sonia. (*She lifts up Sonia's skirt*) They're my knickers!
Sonia Mum gave them to me.
Sarah (*appealing*) Mum!

First Time 55

Sonia (*evil*) I thought they were hers.
Stephen I wanted that LP ever since I saw that live concert.
Grandad Why do they have to argue so. (*To Grandma*) Let's go out for a while.
Jane You only like them because Susan does.
Stephen Nonsense.
Sonia And you only like her because she's got big ...
Julie Sarah! I mean Sonia! That's it, Marvin!
Marvin What?
Julie Will you stop dreaming and speak to your family.
Marvin Hello everyone.
Stephen My LP. My Dire Straits LP.
Sonia I was only playing with the jigsaw.
Jane I think you owe me an apology.
Sarah Fat chance.
Grandad I'm going for a walk.
Grandma No you're not.
Grandad Come with me. The fresh air'll do you good.
Grandma I'm not going outside.
Marvin Right.

Nobody listens. They continue their separate arguments

(*Loudly*) I said "Right"!

Silence

It's Christmas Day. Peace and Goodwill. Our first real family Christmas all together.
Grandad I'm off.
Marvin No you're not.
Grandma You heard him. Sit down.
Marvin We will sort out all these problems and my word will be final.
All Right.

Marvin is pleased he has taken control

Marvin Sonia. Give back Jane's knickers.
Sarah They're *my* knickers.
Marvin Sarah's knickers.
Sonia Oh Mum.
Julie You heard your father. I'll put the kettle on.

Julie exits

Marvin Jane. Did you sit on Stephen's LP?

Sonia storms out

Jane No.
Marvin Sure?
Jane Positive.
Stephen Well someone did.

Grandma I'll buy him another one.
Marvin No you won't.
Grandma Why not?

Stephen storms out

Marvin Sarah. Let Sonia play with your jigsaw.
Sarah Why should I?
Grandma (*still on about the LP*) I can't see why I——
Marvin (*tight-lipped*) Mother. Go for a walk.
Grandma But I don't——
Marvin (*at the end of his tether*) Now!
Grandad You heard him.

The Grandparents leave, Grandma in a huff

Marvin Sarah, let Sonia play with the jigsaw and Jane apologize to Stephen if and when he returns.

Sarah }
Jane } (*together*) But ...

Sarah and Jane storm out

(*Calling after them*) That is, of course, if he hasn't gone to hang himself.

The sound of a door slamming

Then that *would* be dire straits.

Silence. Marvin looks up at the ceiling and speaks quietly

Please Lord, make all future Christmases be more peaceful ... and let Torquay win. Just once. I'm not asking for the FA cup or a place in Europe. Just a win. Thank you.

Julie enters with two cups of tea

Julie Sorted out?
Marvin Sort of.

Julie sits next to Marvin on the sofa

Julie Quiet, isn't it.
Marvin Yes.

They ponder

Julie What are you thinking about? (*She doesn't turn to look at him*)
Marvin (*out front*) Torquay.

Pause

Julie So was I.
Marvin (*turning to look at her*) What?
Julie The first time I met you.
Marvin Oh, at my party.
Julie In your flat. I was drunk. Fast asleep.

First Time

Marvin I asked you to stay.
Julie I was the last to leave.

A slight pause

Marvin You never left.
Julie I did.
Marvin You came back.
Julie I couldn't start the car.

A slight pause

Marvin I hid your keys.

A slight pause

Julie Did you?
Marvin Yes.
Julie You never told me.
Marvin You never asked.

After a while Julie looks at him

Julie Can you remember everything that happened?
Marvin Yes.
Julie Everything?
Marvin Yes. Can you?
Julie Yes, I can. (*She cuddles up closer to him*) I'm just surprised you can.
Marvin Everything. It was . . .

Song: After the Party

(*Singing*)	Late at night and lo
	The guests had gone, had all gone home.
	Daylight was breaking,
	Waking my soul.
	Smoke was hanging high,
	And glasses washed but still not dry.
	I saw you dancing
	Still in your mind.
	Why did you stay,
Julie	I could not say
	Good-night to you.
Marvin	Your keys I'd hid,
Julie	I'm pleased you did,
	I'm glad I stayed that night
	I'm glad I stayed.
Marvin	Didn't speak to you
	Was far too shy to make a move.
Julie	I saw you looking,
	Standing close by.

Both	Everyone had gone
	The music still was playing on.
Marvin	I said, one drink or two
Julie	Will do no harm.
Chorus	Why did you stay,
Marvin ⎱	I could not say
Julie ⎰	Good-night to you.
	Your keys I hid,
	I'm pleased you did,
Julie	I'm glad I stayed that night
	I'm glad I stayed.
Marvin	I'm glad you stayed that night
	I'm glad you stayed.

They cuddle up as the Lights fade

The strobe/freezelite comes on for not more than ten seconds as the Company change for the next scene. Link theme tune "First Time"

Sketch: First Aid

The strobe/freezelite stops and the Lights come up to reveal a street. There has been an accident. An Old Lady has been knocked down by a car. Stephen (Marvin's son) is nursing her. She is lying on the ground but between Stephen's legs so she can rest her head against his thigh. He is cradling her. He is C and facing out front. The Old Lady has her head resting on his left thigh. There is no element of comedy in this sketch

Single tone. We hear a police car disappearing. The freeze is broken. Action and sound start

Old Lady I'm sorry to be a nuisance.
Stephen You're not.
Old Lady I'm a stupid old lady.
Stephen Keep still and don't worry.
Old Lady I didn't see him. I know my eyes are bad but I didn't see him.
Stephen He was going too fast.
Old Lady I should have made sure.

Pause

Stephen Are you comfortable?
Old Lady Yes. (*After a pause*) My legs feel numb.
Stephen They'll be here soon. Somebody's gone to phone.
Old Lady All this fuss.
Stephen Nonsense.
Old Lady (*as she tries to move*) Oh.
Stephen Keep still now.
Old Lady I seem to have hurt my back. (*A slight pause*) I was so annoyed with Sammy.
Stephen You said.

First Time

Old Lady He's usually very good.
Stephen Not to worry.
Old Lady He doesn't usually run off.
Stephen No.
Old Lady He's very naughty. Straight out he ran. I suppose he's in the garden now. Just wait till I see him—causing all this fuss. (*A slight pause*) Can you see him?
Stephen (*after a pause*) No, he's not here.
Old Lady He's a naughty cat.
Stephen Try and keep still.

A slight pause

Old Lady Are you a doctor?
Stephen No.
Old Lady You should be. You're very good.
Stephen I'm an orderly at the local hospital.
Old Lady I see. I thought you might be.
Stephen No.

A slight pause

Old Lady My husband used to say it was the best way to learn a trade. Start at the bottom and work up.
Stephen Yes.
Old Lady I am stupid. A grown woman. I should have known better. (*After a pause*) Do you know how old I am?
Stephen No.
Old Lady Have a guess.
Stephen Late fifties.
Old Lady Don't be silly.
Stephen I'm not very good at ages.
Old Lady Eighty-four.
Stephen No.
Old Lady Eighty-four.
Stephen You don't look it.
Old Lady You'd think at eighty-four I would know better than to walk out into the road without looking wouldn't you?
Stephen It wasn't your fault. He was going too fast.
Old Lady Even so. (*After a pause*) Am I bleeding?

A slight pause

Stephen Just a little.
Old Lady I thought so.
Stephen Hardly anything to worry about.
Old Lady My side feels all sticky.
Stephen It's not much. They'll soon have you back in shape. They're very good.
Old Lady Oh I know. My husband had an operation.
Stephen Did he?

Old Lady Just before he died.
Stephen Oh.
Old Lady He said the doctors were very good. (*After a pause*) What's your name?
Stephen Stephen.
Old Lady Stephen.
Stephen Yes. What's yours?
Old Lady Mrs Smallwood. (*After a pause*) I'm eighty-four. (*A slight pause*) Am I very ill?
Stephen No.
Old Lady I think I am.
Stephen A few cuts and bruises.

A slight pause

Old Lady You're a nice young man. All this fuss. Sammy's very naughty, very naughty.

A long pause

Stephen Mrs Smallwood.
Old Lady You're a nice young man. All this fuss. Sammy's very naughty, very naughty.

A long pause

Stephen Mrs Smallwood. (*After a pause*) Mrs Smallwood.
Old Lady I am a silly old fool. I should know better. (*A slight pause*) How old are you?
Stephen Guess.
Old Lady I can only guess from faces.
Stephen How old do you think?
Old Lady I can't see your face.
Stephen Why not?
Old Lady It's too dark.

He waves his hand in front of her eyes. No reaction

I'm eighty-four.
Stephen Try and rest.
Old Lady Can you see Sammy?
Stephen Not from here.
Old Lady There he is. (*She moves slightly*)
Stephen Try to keep still. They'll be here soon.
Old Lady I can see him behind the rose bush. You naughty boy, all this fuss you've caused, you silly cat. Wait till your Daddy gets home.

A long pause

Stephen Mrs Smallwood. (*After a pause*) Mrs Smallwood. (*A long pause*)

Stephen leans back. Silence. Black-out

First Time

Song: Taking Time

A spot comes up on Sarah L

Sarah Taking time, being kind.
Though you ain't really mine.
Help me meet it and I know
You'll beat it if you stay.

First Time I saw you
Angels adorned you with love
You were sent from up above.
Visions that greet me,
You come to meet me again
Won't you stay until the end.

Chorus La la la

Sarah You're just a friend
Helping to mend
You're a true—friends are hard to come by,
And I don't want to lose you.

People don't seem to take time
To treat you these days
Watch them go their separate ways.
Take joy in caring,
Have faith in sharing your love
We were sent from up above.

Chorus La la la

The strobe/freezelite comes on for not more than ten seconds as the Company change for the next scene

  Stephen and the Old Lady leave the area

Link theme tune "First Time"

Sketch: First Medical

The strobe/freezelite stops and the Lights come up to reveal Marvin in the Doctor's consulting room. He is in his shorts and vest. Marvin is getting dressed but neither is listening to the other. The Doctor is writing notes. Their dialogue almost overlaps

Single tone. The freeze is broken. Action and sound start

Doctor Do you sleep well at night?
Marvin No trouble—like a log.
Doctor Yes, well I'll give you these pills and you'll find they'll help you to sleep at night . . .

Marvin I still get nightmares . . .
Doctor . . . what you need is a good rest . . .
Marvin . . . I think it's because I get tired all the time . . .
Doctor . . . a complete rest. Take a holiday . . .
Marvin . . . Tom reckons it's pressure . . .
Doctor . . . and if those pains in your arm . . .
Marvin . . . I don't feel pressured . . .
Doctor . . . don't get any better . . .
Marvin . . . just funny . . .
Doctor . . . come back and see me, OK?
Marvin . . . Julie says I look terrible . . .
Doctor Good.
Marvin Good!! (*Disgusted—listening to the Doctor for the first time*)
Doctor Next!
Marvin Thanks very much! That's all I need. You telling me I look terrible as well.

The Doctor goes head down as he flicks through cards to find the next patient's details. He thinks Marvin has gone

A Woman enters

Marvin talks to himself as he dresses

I mean, when you feel like I feel, the last thing you want is your nearest and dearest——

The Woman realizes that Marvin is dressing and is about to go out

—telling you you look terrible.
Doctor (*without looking up*) Come in. Sit down.

Throughout the ensuing dialogue, the Doctor is aware of the Woman, but not of Marvin, who in turn is not aware of the Woman

Name?
Marvin (*before the Woman can answer*) Marvin Tadler. I mean I suppose I've had certain pressures. Work. Little bit of overtime. But nothing out of the ordinary.
Doctor Sweater.

He signals to the Woman to remove her top. She is a little nervous to do so in front of Marvin

Marvin No more than anyone else. Little perspiration under the armpits. That sort of thing.
Doctor (*impatient with the Woman*) Come along.
Marvin All right. I'm going as fast as I can.
Doctor (*to the woman*) Sniff.

She does so

Marvin (*socks in hand, sniffing them*) Blimey, they're a bit bad aren't they?

First Time

Throughout, the Woman has her eyes closed in embarrassment. The Doctor is still not aware of Marvin, and Marvin is not aware of the Woman

Doctor (*to the Woman*) Cough.

She does so

Marvin Well, not to mention. I've never been a smoker—anything daft like that.
Doctor (*to the Woman referring to the sweater*) Put it back on.
Marvin (*looking at his sock*) Right. (*He puts it on*) Mind you I don't think any of that accounts of these dreadful nightmares. I thought it might be the kids arguing all the time or——

The Doctor writes a prescription for the Woman

—maybe the continuous stream of bills I can't pay.
Doctor (*handing a prescription to the Woman*) Three times a day.
Marvin That's what it seems like.
Doctor First thing in the morning.
Marvin Yes, always get one with the breakfast.
Doctor Midday.
Marvin Every post there seems to be a bill.
Doctor And before you go to bed.
Marvin I'm glad you understand, Doctor. I'm glad somebody understands.

The Woman exits hurriedly

I suppose the TV licence will be next. (*Pulling on this shoes*) All that money just to watch drivel. Be honest, when was the last time you watched Match of the Day? No wonder I have funny turns. Take last week. I had this dreadful nightmare when I came face to face with the devil! I mean that's really daft innit? (*Now dressed*) What do you think?
Doctor Next?
Marvin Doctor?

The Doctor looks up thinking Marvin has returned

Doctor Ah, Mr Tadler. Still feeling no better?

Marvin looks out to the audience. Freeze. Black-out, during which Marvin exits

Pause. We hear the first chords of "First to Fall"

Satan appears on a high level UL. *The cyclorama is flooded red*

Song: First to Fall

Satan   I'm the one that makes you hate,
           I'm the one that makes you take.
           I'm the one that wants your soul,
           If it's black I'll take control.
           I was the first to fall.

	I'm the one that God forsake, I'm the one, yes, the big mistake. I'm the serpent that lurks below, I'm the power that the wicked know. I was the first to fall.
Chorus	I am the corruption, yes, I am that vile eruption That will keep the fires burning down below. Mortals now tread carefully For I am not that heavenly, And once I have you down I don't let go.
Satan	I'm the one that makes you blind, Vice and Sin are friends of mine. If you stray then God will see, I'll have you for eternity. I was the first to fall. Give me souls and in return, All your troubles I WILL BURN. Evil is my power base, Darkness is my kindly face. I was the first to fall.
Chorus	I am the corruption, yes, I am that vile eruption That will keep the fires burning down below. Mortals now tread carefully For I am not that heavenly, And once I have you down I don't let go.

The strobe/freezelite comes on for not more than ten seconds as the Company change for the next scene. Over the moves, we hear ghostly echoing words "Marvin Tadler, Marvin Tadler-er-er-er". Link theme tune "First Time"

Sketch: First Offence

The strobe/freezelite stops and the Lights come up to reveal a heavenly courtroom. A Judge sits very high up C assisted by a saucy secretary Miss Twee. The Jury sits at an angle L, an assorted bunch. Between the Judge and the Jury slightly forward is a table where Dobbs, prosecuting counsel and Syms, defending counsel sit. R there is a witness box. The inside of the box is being dusted by a Cleaner. Note: All the Jury's hats and the Judge's wig are attached to thin fishing line. They do not leave their positions during the sketch. At the end these hats and wigs fly off in a fast comical fashion

Single tone. The freeze is broken. Action and sound start

We are in Marvin's nightmare. His first offence is to be judged. The courtroom is noisy when the freeze breaks until the judge silences them

Judge (*banging his hammer*) Silence. (*To the Cleaner*) You are Marvin Tadler of Nutleigh Grove, Basildon?

First Time

Cleaner (*popping up from the witness box*) No.
Judge Well, that's not a very good start is it?
Cleaner I'm the cleaner.
Judge Well get on with your work.
Cleaner Right. (*To the audience*) Good here, ain't it?
Jury Yeah!

The Cleaner exits

Judge Silence! Mr Dobbs.
Dobbs Sorry, my Lord. The prosecution calls for the accused. Mr Marvin Tadler.

A Policeman calls off-stage

PC Calling Mr Marvin Tadler.
Twee Shall I take all this down, Your Honour?
Judge Not at the moment Miss Twee. For now, just write out what's said.

Marvin enters

PC Marvin Tadler, Your Honour.
Judge You are Mr Marvin Tadler of Nutleigh Grove, Basildon?
Marvin It's not worth lying I suppose?
Judge Certainly not.
Marvin In that case I am he.
Judge Good. Proceed Mr Dobbs.
Dobbs Before I call the first witness I'd like to put a few questions to the accused.
Judge Very well.

A professional pause

Dobbs Did you murder him?

A slight pause

Marvin Who?
Dobbs I think you know who I mean Mr Tadler. You surely don't think that the jury will fall for any cock and bull story about "I was not feeling myself at the time" or "Dole depression" or "I am a sign of the times".
Marvin I don't understand.
Dobbs So you say, but I think you do—and I repeat, did you murder him?
Syms (*the defence counsel*) I object.
Judge So do I Mr Dobbs. Is this line of questioning really relevant to one's failure to pay one's TV licence?
Dobbs I think, My Lord, I will soon uncover a plot, yes, a plot so sinister that not even Mr Tadler here knew of it.
Judge Oh very well.
Dobbs Let me put it another way. Did you murder him?
Marvin Who?
Dobbs Very well. Let me take you back to the day of the offence.
Marvin My first offence.

Dobbs As you say, your first offence. You were approached by two men who resembled a North-country double act. Correct?

The ensuing dialogue goes like machine-gun fire

Marvin Correct.
Dobbs They asked you to produce your TV licence.
Marvin But I couldn't.
Dobbs Because?
Marvin I didn't have one.
Dobbs They said...
Marvin We'll prosecute.
Dobbs You said...
Marvin Oh bloody hell.
Dobbs And they...
Marvin Walked away.
Dobbs And you...
Marvin Shut the door.
Dobbs And...
Marvin That was all.
Dobbs But was it?
Marvin Yes!

They revert to normal. Dobbs looks around the court knowingly. He's a show-off and plays everything as if he is in a "soap" legal drama. He picks up some papers

Dobbs Did one of these men happen to mention the climate?
Marvin What?
Dobbs The weather Mr Tadler, the weather.
Marvin Might have done.
Dobbs One of them did in fact say (*he reads from the paper*) "Lovely weather we're having" (*he looks up*) and you said "Not bad".
Marvin So. Nothing wrong with that.
Dobbs As you say Mr Tadler, nothing wrong with that.
Syms Your Honour!
Judge (*as if caught doing something with Miss Twee*) No I'm not! (*He pushes Miss Twee away*)
Syms I object.
Judge So do I. Where is this leading to Mr Dobbs?
Dobbs All, Your Honour, will soon be clear.
Twee It's just like "Dallas".
Judge Is it? Well get on with it.
Dobbs Did you not then notice something *crawling* on the ground!?
Marvin I don't think so. (*He is becoming nervous*)
Dobbs And was this thing *crawling* on the ground not a—spider!?
Marvin I can't remember. (*He panics*)
Dobbs A very small harmless spider innocently going about its business.

Murmurs from the court

First Time

Marvin No I didn't see him, I tell yer. I didn't see him.
Dobbs Did you not Mr Tadler, stand on that spider and squash him to death!
Marvin No! No! No! It was a mistake!

General outburst

Judge Order! order! Restrain the prisoner.
Marvin It was an accident.
Dobbs Accident! Accident! I put it to you Mr Marvin Tadler of Nutleigh Grove, Basildon, that you, in a fit of revenge, incensed at being caught in the act of TV licence avoidance, callously—and I do not use that term loosely, callously (*with an intake of breath*) trod on that spider!
Syms I object My Lord.
Dobbs Just as you once did previously in the playground of your old school when you were a juvenile spider offender. Isn't that right, Marvin Tadler!
Syms My Lord!

Outburst

Judge Mr Dobbs I hope you have evidence to support this serious and unprecedented attack on Mr Syms's client.
Dobbs I have, My Lord.

The Judge confers with clerk. Outburst

Judge Order! Order!

Silence

Continue Mr Dobbs.
Dobbs The prosecution would like to call to the stand Constable Matthews.
PC Constable Matthews! Constable Matthews!
Dobbs That's you, you fool.
PC Oh yes. Sorry My Lord. (*He enters the witness box*)
Dobbs Would you swear on the Bible please.
PC (*his hand on the Bible, speaking respectfully*) Knickers! (*or "Bloody Hell!"*)
Dobbs Thank you. Now can you tell the court what you did on Monday July seventh, nineteen eighty-five.
PC Certainly. I awoke at approximately six-thirty a.m. and got up to clean my teeth, wash and shave which was followed by a hearty breakfast of Kelloggs' Poppa Pops.
Dobbs Concerning this case Constable, that's all. And in your own words.
PC Of course. I was walking my beat ... (*his memory is not good and he is fed the words surreptitiously by Dobbs. He does this in all sorts of funny ways, alternately soft and loud*)
Dobbs (*soft*) Close to Nutleigh Grove.
PC (*loud*) Close to Nutleigh Grove.
Dobbs When a young boy ...
PC When a young boy ...
Dobbs Of about seven ...

PC Of about seven . . .
Dobbs Told me he had lost his pet spider Hercules.
PC Told me he had lost his pet spider Hercules.
Dobbs At that moment I heard a voice shout . . .
PC At that moment I heard a voice shout . . .
Dobbs (*shouting*) "Take that you bastard!"
PC (*shouting*) "Take that you bastard!"
Dobbs "Who d'you think you're grinning at?"
PC "Who d'you think you're grinning at?"
Dobbs (*normal voice*) And is the owner of that voice present in this court?
PC And is the owner of that . . .

Dobbs points at Marvin

Er yes, it is the accused.
Dobbs Continue.
PC I then said (*he reads from a notebook*): "Now my lad, you'd better come along with me——"
Dobbs Thank you. You see My Lord—— (*He moves away from the box but turns back when the PC speaks*)
PC "—please——"
Dobbs Thank you——(*He moves away. Repeat action*)
PC "—and he did."
Dobbs All right. (*He smiles at the court*) That will be all thank you.
Judge Witness may step down.
PC Oh. (*To the audience—disappointed*) I was quite enjoying that.
Dobbs No more witnesses My Lord.
PC (*to the audience*) Bit nervous to start with but . . .

Everyone stares at the PC who senses his presence is no longer required and slinks into a corner

Judge Mr Syms

Syms stands

Syms Thank you My Lord. I would now, ladies and gentlemen of the jury, like to unravel this web of intrigue spun by my learned colleague, this complex cacophany of claptrap, this jumble of judicious drivel, this——
Judge Get on with it.
Syms Of course. Would you describe yourself as a ruthless man Mr Tadler?
Marvin No.
Syms A hard man?
Marvin Not really.
Syms A family man?
Marvin Wife and three kids.
Syms A kindly man?
Marvin Sort of.
Syms Do you hate people?
Marvin (*smiling*) I love them.
Syms What about animals?

First Time

Marvin (*smiling*) What about them?
Syms Fond of them?
Marvin (*nervy*) In what way?
Syms Have you any pets?
Marvin Few.
Syms Dog?
Marvin Cat.
Syms Hamster?
Marvin Gerbil.
Syms Tortoise?
Marvin Rabbit.
Syms Any more?
Marvin Well . . .
Syms Go on. Any pets you are particularly fond of?
Marvin Yes. (*After a slight pause*) Cornelius.
Syms And Cornelius is?
Marvin A spider.
Syms A spider?
Marvin Yes.
Syms A spider?
Marvin (*after a pause*) Yes.
Syms (*to the Jury*) Ladies and gentlemen of the jury, are we expected to believe that a man who is married with two children and a house full of pets, in particular, a spider name Cornelius, could, to use my learned colleague's term, callously kill Hercules? (*Pause for effect*) Hercules, who could have been a brother of Cornelius. A sister perhaps?
PC Or a long-lost cousin.

All look at him in disgust

Syms (*after a slight pause*) Is it really possible that Mr Tadler, an engineer——

The PC hands him a slip of paper from which he reads out loud

——and "part-time Avon lady" could, by any stretch of the imagination squash the guts out of a harmless little spider?

He sits. Dobbs stands

Dobbs (*with a smirk*) Is Cornelius here now?
Marvin What?
Dobbs Where is Cornelius?
Marvin At home.
Dobbs At home? At home? I thought you said you were fond of Cornelius?
Marvin I am.
Dobbs But you left him at home?
Marvin Yes.
Dobbs On an important day like today, your first court case. Didn't you want him to be with you to share this moment?
Marvin I——

Dobbs I put it to you Mr Tadler, that Cornelius doesn't exist.
Marvin It does.
Dobbs Miss Twee.

Miss Twee brings him a matchbox

I have here a friendly little spider.

She screams, stands on a chair and pulls up her skirt

It's all right Miss Twee. It's on a lead.

She lets down her skirt but he likes what he has seen

But only a very thin lead.

She screams again and pulls up her skirt

Judge Get on with it Dobbs!
Dobbs (*placing the spider near Marvin*) Look at him Mr Tadler.
Marvin (*pulling back*) Why should I?
Dobbs Because you like them.
Marvin So what?
Dobbs You look nervous Mr Tadler.
Marvin No.
Dobbs Almost frightened.
Marvin I don't see why . . .
Dobbs Why don't you stroke him Mr Tadler? You've just told the court what a great love of spiders you have.
Marvin Spiders?
Dobbs Remember Cornelius?
Marvin Cornelius?
Dobbs I do believe he's grinning.
Marvin What? (*He sweats*)
Dobbs Yes look Mr Tadler. He's grinning at you.
Marvin No!
Dobbs Yes!
Marvin No! No!
Dobbs Yes!
Marvin I can't stand it! I can't stand it!
Dobbs What on earth's wrong Mr Tadler?
Marvin Who do you think you're grinning at? (*He glares at the spider*) I'll teach you you bastard. Take that—(*he smacks the spider with the flat of his hand*)—and that and that!

Silence. Marvin slowly looks up at the court who are sitting absolutely still and open-mouthed at his sudden outburst

Dobbs No further questions My Lord.
Judge Marvin Tadler, do you have anything to say before I pass judgement, having condemned yourself with your own actions!
Marvin No.
Judge Very well then. I sentence you to——

First Time 71

Swanee whistle sound and all hats and wigs fly off as court and contents spin off the area in a dreamlike fashion

The strobe/freezelite comes on for not more than ten seconds as the Company change for the next scene. Link theme tune "First Time"

Sketch: First Death

The strobe/freezelite stops and the Lights come up to reveal Tom coming from L on his way home from work and Marvin standing C. Marvin has a toolbag in his hand and Tom carries an evening paper

Single tone. The freeze is broken. Action and sound start. Tom starts to walk past Marvin. Marvin looks up dazed

Tom Marvin. Just finished your shift?
Marvin Evening Tom. Yes, just finished.
Tom You all right?
Marvin Little bit under the weather that's all. I had a funny turn.
Tom Thought I'd see you smirking all over your face.
Marvin Why?
Tom "Why", he says.
Marvin Tom I'm not in the mood for games. I don't feel that great mate.
Tom You don't look it.
Marvin That's because I'm not.
Tom (*amused*) You really don't know do you?
Marvin Know what?
Tom About Torquay.
Marvin What about Torquay?

Tom shakes his head in disbelief

Tom Have you got a paper?
Marvin You're not going to do some more of that origami nonsense are you?
Tom Have you got a paper?
Marvin No. I have not got a paper.

Tom hands him his evening paper

Tom Take mine.
Marvin What for?
Tom (*moving off*) See you tomorrow.
Marvin (*calling after Tom*) Why have you given me your paper?
Tom (*shouting back as he leaves*) Read the sports page.

Tom exits

Marvin Read the ... (*Suddenly his face brightens with realization. He searches frantically through the paper until he finds what he's looking for. Pause, then he looks up*) They've won.

We hear the first chord of "First to Fall". Marvin stiffens, wide-eyed. Freeze.

The first chord is repeated. Marvin is transfixed. His mouth is open, his eyes stare. We hear the ghostly voices of his past coming from those characters on their chairs

Sally Paul, it's coming.

A slight pause

June Your name Marvin?

The first chord again. During the following lines he starts to collapse in very slow motion to the floor, still clutching the paper and looking out. The following lines may be pre-recorded with Marvin's voice on or spoken by Stephen as his father. Marvin should not have collapsed fully until the final "Yes"

Officer Have you had a job, Marvin?
Marvin I had a job to get up this morning.
Officer It's not a bed of pansies I can tell you.
Marvin's Voice Ladies, may I have the pleasure?
Julie Hello. I'm sorry I'm late.
Marvin's Voice What would you like to do tonight?
Julie Have you got to the bit about the donkey?
Marvin's Voice Easy. Alucard Eripmaff is Dracula Ffampire spelt backwards.
Alucard Kill joy.
Photographer I'll just check my camera.
Julie's Mum He won't be in there.
Julie Marvin!
Sarah Mum, Jane's got my knickers.
Stephen My Dire Straits LP.
Julie Marvin will you talk to them.
Sonia Dad.
Jane Mum.
Julie Marvin!
Marvin's Voice Please Lord, let Torquay win, just once.
Julie The first time I met you.
Marvin's Voice At my party.
Julie I couldn't start the car.
Marvin's Voice I hid your keys.
Julie Can you remember everything that happened?
Marvin's Voice Yes.
Julie Everything?
Marvin's Voice Yes.

Marvin has now collapsed. Pause

Everything.

Pause. God has appeared on a raised level upstage R. *The cyclorama is flooded with bright light*

First Time

Song: First to Fall (Reprise)

God   I'm the one that will decide,
Satan, now just stand aside.
Where his soul will finally go
Only I can really know——
I was the first of all——
If his heart is black and stained
And all the goodness has been drained.
Take him then with no delay
But I will have the final say——
I was the first of all.

Chorus   I am the redemption, yes, I am the soul collection
For all those that fought temptation down below.
Mortals now tread carefully
For he is not that heavenly,
And once he has you down he won't let go.

The Lights fade slowly to a spot on Marvin, which then fades slowly. Darkness. Strobe effect

Company curtain call to reprise of "First Time"

FURNITURE AND PROPERTY LIST

On stage throughout:
    Chairs for each member of the Company—personal props can be on, hanging from or under these chairs—see Production Notes

FIRST HALF

Song: First Time

No props required

Sketch: First Child

On stage: Bus stop

Personal: **Policeman:** two-way radio
          Docker: bag, watch

Song: Baby

On stage: Baby for **Sally** and **Paul**

Off stage: 3 babies in blankets **(Mothers)**
          Babies **(Girls)**
          Prams, pushchairs **(Men)**

Personal: **Mother:** papoose
          Marvin: spectacles

Sketch: First Fag

Off stage: Tennis balls, rackets **(Nutty Norman** and **gang)**

Personal: **Marvin:** spectacles, packet of cigarettes, matches

Song: Can You Remember?

Off stage: Tennis rackets **(Norman's gang)**

Sketch: First Job

On stage: Small bench
          Display board with posters
          Small table. *On it:* papers, pen, intercom, pamphlets
          Chair
          Cup of tea for **Doreen**

Off stage: Cup of tea **(Doreen)**
          Glass of water, aspirin **(Doreen)**

Personal: **Officer:** spectacles
          Marvin: spectacles

First Time

Sketch: First Night

On stage: 2 tables. *On them:* make-up
  Dora's table. *On it:* bottles, tablets, vase of water
  Screen
  Chairs
  Costumes
  Props for **Rene**

Off stage: Flowers **(Pat)**
  Chair **(Rene)**
  Bottle **(Marvin)**

Personal: **Marvin:** spectacles

Song: First Glance

On stage: Bench
  Lamppost

Personal: **Marvin:** spectacles, watch, small box with necklace
  Marvin's Girl: make-up, mirror
  Girl-friend: chewing gum

Sketch: First Kiss/Glance

On stage: Bench
  "Keep Off the Grass" sign
  "Public Park" sign
  Waste-bin

Off stage: Paper-wrapped chips **(Old Gertie)**

Personal: **Tom:** watch
  Marvin: photograph, spectacles in pocket
  Julie: letter, spectacles in case

Song: A Woman

Personal: **Marvin:** spectacles
  Julie: spectacles

Sketch: First Bite

On stage: Piano and stool.
  Throne-like chair draped in gauze

Off stage: Storybook **(Narrator)**
  Bicycle wheel **(Marvin)**
  Rolling pin, flour **(Alucard)**
  Bicycles **(2 Maids)**
  Wooden stake, mallet **(Marvin)**

Personal: **Butler:** photograph
  Company: books, playing cards, etc.; umbrellas

SECOND HALF

Song: First Time (Reprise)

No props required

Song: First Time I Saw You

On stage: Sid's coat on back of chair

Personal: **Girl 1:** huge feet, black teeth, bag
Girl 2: hump
Norman: mac and cap
Julie: engagement ring
Marvin: buttonhole on pocket

Sketch: First Wife

Off stage: Ice-lollies **(Bridesmaids)**
Camera **(Photographer)**

Personal: **Marvin's Dad:** buttonhole, hip flask
Best Man, Julie's Dad: buttonholes
Julie, Bridesmaids: bouquets
Photographer: business card

Song: We Are Just Beginning

No props required

Sketch: First Family Christmas

On stage: Table. *On it:* jigsaw
Fire
Sofa
Chairs
Knitting for **Julie**

Off stage: 2 cups of tea **(Julie)**

Personal: **All:** party hats
Marvin: pipe

Sketch: First Aid

No props required

Song: Taking Time

No props required

Sketch: First Medical

On stage: Desk. *On it:* patients' cards, pen, prescription pad
2 chairs. *On one:* **Marvin**'s clothes

Song: First to Fall

No props required

Sketch: First Offence

On stage: High desk and chair. *On desk:* hammer, matchbox with spider
Seats for **Jury**
Table. *On table:* papers
Chairs
Witness box. *In it:* Bible
Duster for **Cleaner**

Personal: **Judge, Jury:** wig and hats attached to thin fishing line
PC: notebook, slip of paper

Sketch: First Death

Personal: **Marvin:** toolbag
Tom: evening paper

LIGHTING PLOT

FIRST HALF

Cue 1	When ready *Houselights out; slowly bring up lighting until* **Company** *are in position; then snap up to full general lighting on main playing area*	(Page 1)
Cue 2	At end of Song: First Time *Strobe or freezelite for ten seconds; then lights up on Sketch: First Child—a bus stop*	(Page 2)
Cue 3	**Sally/Paul** (*singing*): "For more than that/It's ..." *Snap up spot on* **Marvin**	(Page 10)
Cue 4	**All** (*in total disgust*): "Eeeeeaaaaarrrrch!" *Strobe/freezelite; then lights up on Sketch: First Fag—a playground*	(Page 11)
Cue 5	At end of Song: Can You Remember? *Strobe/freezelite for ten seconds; then lights up on Sketch: First Job—an office*	(Page 18)
Cue 6	**Officer:** "I know what I mean." *Black-out; then strobe/freezelite for ten seconds; then lights up on Sketch: First Night—a dressing room*	(Page 22)
Cue 7	**Officer:** "Exactly." **Marvin:** "Right." *Strobe/freezelite for ten seconds; then lights up on Song: First Glance, with spot on lamppost*	(Page 27)
Cue 8	At end of Song: First Glance *Fade lights on* **Marvin**; *then strobe/freezelite for ten seconds; then lights up on Sketch: First Kiss—a park*	(Page 29)
Cue 9	**Marvin** puts on his glasses and **Julie** moves towards him *Fade to a tight spot on* **Marvin** *and* **Julie**	(Page 35)
Cue 10	As **Marvin** watches **Julie** go *Fade slowly to black-out; pause, then bring up general lighting*	(Page 35)
Cue 11	**Marvin:** "... had found 'true love'." *Strobe/freezelite for ten seconds; then lights up on Sketch: First Bite—a castle interior—spooky lighting*	(Page 35)
Cue 12	**Narrator** enters L *Spot on* **Narrator**	(Page 35)
Cue 13	**Narrator:** "... that awaited them ..." *Green light on* **Narrator**	(Page 36)

First Time   79

Cue 14	**Narrator** exits	(Page 36)
	Cut green spot; flash of lightning	
Cue 15	As **Julie** opens imaginary window curtains	(Page 43)
	Brighten lights	
Cue 16	As **Alucard** closes imaginary window curtains	(Page 43)
	Return to previous level	
Cue 17	As **Company** exit	(Page 44)
	Strobe effect until stage is clear	

SECOND HALF

To open: Lighting on **Marvin** and **Julie**

Cue 18	At end of Song: First Time (Reprise)	(Page 45)
	Strobe/freezelite for ten seconds; then lights up on Song: First Time I Saw You—a street	
Cue 19	At end of Song: First Time I Saw You	(Page 47)
	Strobe/freezelite for ten seconds; then lights up on Sketch: First Wife—outside a church	
Cue 20	At end of Song: We Are Just Beginning	(Page 52)
	Strobe/freezelite for ten seconds; then lights up on Sketch: First Family Christmas—a living-room	
Cue 21	At end of Song: After the Party	(Page 58)
	Fade lights; then strobe/freezelite for ten seconds; then lights up on Sketch: First Aid—a street	
Cue 22	**Stephen** leans back. Silence	(Page 60)
	Black-out	
Cue 23	When ready	(Page 61)
	Bring up spot on **Sarah** L	
Cue 24	At end of Song: Taking Time	(Page 61)
	Strobe/freezelite for ten seconds; then lights up on Sketch: First Medical—a doctor's consulting room	
Cue 25	**Marvin** looks out to audience. Freeze	(Page 63)
	Black-out	
Cue 26	When ready	(Page 63)
	Red lighting on cyclorama	
Cue 27	At end of Song: First to Fall	(Page 64)
	Strobe/freezelite for ten seconds; then lights up on Sketch: First Offence—a courtroom	
Cue 28	After court and contents spin off area in a dreamlike fashion	(Page 71)
	Strobe/freezelite for ten seconds; then lights up on Sketch: First Death—a street	
Cue 29	**God** appears UR	(Page 72)
	Flood cyclorama with bright lighting	

Cue 30	At end of Song: First to Fall (Reprise)	(Page 73)
	Fade slowly to spot on **Marvin**; *then slowly fade spot to black-out; then strobe effect*	
Cue 31	When ready	(Page 73)
	Cut strobe effect; bring up lights for reprise of Song: First Time	

EFFECTS PLOT

FIRST HALF

Cue 1	After lights come up on Sketch: First Child *Single tone*	(Page 2)
Cue 2	**Policeman:** "Very well Sandra." *Bus approaches and then departs*	(Page 6)
Cue 3	As Sketch: First Fag begins *Handbell rings, with noises of kids messing about, off*	(Page 11)
Cue 4	After lights come up on Sketch: First Job *Single tone*	(Page 18)
Cue 5	As **Doreen** enters with cup of tea then exits *Stripper music*	(Page 19)
Cue 6	As **Doreen** enters with water and aspirin then exits *Stripper music*	(Page 20)
Cue 7	After lights come up on Sketch: First Night *Single tone*	(Page 22)
Cue 8	After lights come up on Song: First Glance *Single tone*	(Page 27)
Cue 9	After lights come up on Sketch: First Kiss *Single tone*	(Page 29)
Cue 10	After lights come up on Sketch: First Bite *Single tone*	(Page 35)
Cue 11	**Narrator** exits *Clap of thunder*	(Page 36)
Cue 12	**Marvin** rings "doorbell" *British Telecom telephone rings*	(Page 36)
Cue 13	**Butler** opens "door" slightly *Creaking sound*	(Page 36)
Cue 14	**Butler:** "Please come in." *Very loud sound of huge door creaking opening*	(Page 37)
Cue 15	**Butler:** "Esmerelda!" *Clatter of bells being dropped, off*	(Page 37)
Cue 16	**Alucard** opens the creaking door *Repeat Cue 14*	(Page 39)
Cue 17	**Alucard:** "On your bike!" *Door slams*	(Page 39)

Cue 18	**Alucard** door *Short, sharp creak*	(Page 40)
Cue 19	As **Marvin** hits stake *Hollow sound*	(Page 44)
Cue 20	**Marvin:** "So ends his dreadful reign." *Clap of thunder, rain effect*	(Page 44)

SECOND HALF

Cue 21	After lights come up on Song: First Time I Saw You *Single tone*	(Page 45)
Cue 22	After lights come up on Sketch: First Wife *Hymn plays off; then single tone*	(Page 47)
Cue 23	**Vicar** enters church *Classical tune plays, off*	(Page 47)
Cue 24	**Marvin's Dad:** "... in the first place." *Funeral march plays, off*	(Page 48)
Cue 25	**Best Man:** "Here they come again." *Organ plays "She Loves You", off*	(Page 49)
Cue 26	**Julie's Mum** enters with the kindly consoling **Sister** *Organ plays "Rock Around the Clock"*	(Page 49)
Cue 27	**Julie's Mum:** "He looks drunk to me." *Organ plays hit tune, off*	(Page 50)
Cue 28	**Photographer:** "Charming." *Discordant chord on organ, then lid slams*	(Page 51)
Cue 29	Everyone exits into church *Organ plays "Here Comes the Bride"*	(Page 51)
Cue 30	After lights come up on Sketch: First Family Christmas *Christmas carol plays in background; fade after a few seconds; then single tone*	(Page 52)
Cue 31	**Marvin:** "... gone to hang himself." *Door slams off*	(Page 56)
Cue 32	After lights come up on Sketch: First Aid *Single tone; then sound of police car disappearing*	(Page 58)
Cue 33	After lights come up on Sketch: First Medical *Single tone*	(Page 61)
Cue 34	As Company change for Sketch: First Offence *Ghostly echoing words "Marvin Tadler, Marvin Tadler-er-er-er"*	(Page 64)
Cue 35	After lights come up on Sketch: First Offence *Single tone*	(Page 64)
Cue 36	**Judge:** "I sentence you to——" *Swanee whistle as all hats and wings fly off*	(Page 71)
Cue 37	After lights come up on Sketch: First Death *Single tone*	(Page 71)

www.ingramcontent.com/pod-product-compliance
Ingram Content Group UK Ltd.
Pitfield, Milton Keynes, MK11 3LW, UK
UKHW021842140426
5217IPUK00022B/1551

9 780573 080739